A Year in Ink
Volume 7

I0659127

San Diego Writers, Ink

A Year in Ink

ANTHOLOGY VOLUME 7

Edited by

Shadab Zeest Hashmi and Jim Ruland

THE
INK SPOT
PRESS

San Diego, California

A Year in Ink, Volume 7 is a publication of
The Ink Spot Press
San Diego Writers, Ink
NTC at Liberty Station
2730 Historic Decatur Rd.
Barracks 16, Suite 202
San Diego, CA 92106

Many thanks go to our many first readers and hardworking
proofreaders. Special thanks to Sumilu Cue, Kristen Fogle, Janene
Roberts, and Kim Keeline for their efforts.

Cover image:
"Wave Break" by Dave Ness
www.DaveNessPhotography.com

Cover and layout and design:
Golden Ratio Design
www.GoldenRatio.anthonybonds.com

ISBN: 978-0-9799204-6-2
Printed in the United States of America
Printed by Lightning Source Inc.

Contents

Introduction by
Shadab Zeest Hashmi
and Jim Ruland

W E ARE WRITING TODAY NOT AS writers but as readers. We read for all kinds of reasons, but one of the main pleasures of reading is the extraordinary feeling of being surprised. As readers we are always looking for that feeling. An elegant turn of phrase. A harrowing problem. A comical solution. We laugh and cry and stay up late so that we can keep turning the pages. It's the surprise that makes us catch our breath and stays with us after our reading is done.

If the writer does his or her job well, we forget all about them and delve into the world they have created with their words. But as editors we can't forget about the writers. Although we read the submissions blind, we were always aware that when our role as readers was done, we would have to make some very difficult decisions to make as editors.

In addition to being readers and editors, we are writers, too. We know what it's like to send one's work off to be judged and, more often than not, to be disappointment by that judgment. The majority of the time we are sending our work off to journals in magazines in other cities, other states, and other countries, to places where we are not known.

That's not the case with this anthology, a book for San Diegans by San Diegans. Those who are published in *A Year in Ink Volume 7* can expect to be read by their friends and family, their coworkers and colleagues. These writers might run into their readers at the coffee shop or while out for a stroll on the beach. Writers and readers everywhere you look.

We were struck again and again by the courage of those who submitted their work, to not only share their poetry and prose with us, but to offer them up to be judged again, and again and again. We are proud to live in a community that produces writers of such fearlessness. Each time we were reminded of it, we would have some very difficult decisions to make as editors.

We thank each and every writer who submitted work to the anthology. Whether you're a beginning writer just starting out or a seasoned veteran with many publications under your belt, we appreciate the opportunity to enter a new world full of surprises. We are better readers, and our experience has been enlarged because of it.

We'd also like to thank all the volunteers at San Diego Writers, Ink—past and present—whose tireless efforts result in a book that everyone can be proud to share with the literary community.

Lastly, we'd like to thank the San Diego Writers, Ink board of directors and its staff, and especially Kristen Fogle who reassured us that we knew what we were doing.

It gives us great pleasure to present *A Year in Ink Volume 7*. It is our hope that you enjoy reading it as much as we did putting it together. You just might surprise yourself and feel inspired to write something for next year's anthology.

              —SHADAB ZEEST HASHMI & JIM RULAND

San Diego Writers, Ink

A Year in Ink

ANTHOLOGY VOLUME 7

Touching the Past

Claudia Poquoc

Time past lingers
from ancient fingers
scraping the surface of
igneous rock. A world forgotten—
only shards of memory exist
in our present ruin.

Rock speaks:

"Once, no longer content to hunt and eat,
your kind sought a talisman—
wished forth a wick.

The Igniter fired your thought.
Rock glyphs were brought to life.
You pecked tattoos into the cortex
of my skin to record your way to eternity.

Chiseled with deer antler, etched with
cactus juice, symbols sprouted like fine
grain in nature-filled skull sockets.
All that you pressed, impressed you.

While scarring indentations over basalt skin,
you sensed the lava that I had once been.
Then a sunrise pierced night's shadow
spearing your mark. Meaning dawned in you.

What were you calling with your Tap... Tap... Tap?
Was it to craft the antelope into your snare?

Tap! Tap! Was it to open shamanic doors to the
underworld? Tap! Tap! Was it to re-open
an earth slit from which you emerged?

Etched with riddles that only I am old enough to rhyme,
you, in your infancy, must have wondered at the yucca
apron that once covered your mother's mound and how
culture began when a very old virgin started to bleed."

The Monarch

Claudia Poquoc

"Why search for a core in an onion?" I ask my 100 year old mother who is still seeking answers with which to line her coffin. "Come sit with me in the garden. I am a self-appointed midwife protecting some fantastic rebirths while my two whiskered marauders are on patrol. Watch and wait with me while eight glassy serpent-green cocoons dangle from obscure places: from a dried twig, on the underside of weathered plant stand, from the lip of a cactus planter—all suspended from single silk filaments. See how gold beads circle the neck of each chrysalis while inside, a sorcerer's soup is brewing. Out of this mini caldron slips a whole other radiant being with fire-orange wings and ink brush veins. As each slides out of its gauzy dream sac, time stops. So come, mother, sit with me. Together we will wait until this human notion for security releases its grip on your unfolding wings."

a caterpillar dreams
out slips my mother
no words for it

Aikoku Maru

Lynn Bemiller

J OYLEEN FOLLOWED TWO RESPECTFUL STEPS BEHIND Mr. Imwao, the hospital administrator, as he escorted the latest band of visitors through the town hospital.

On an ordinary day, touring with foreign dignitaries was assuredly not a job for middle-aged ward nurses like Joyleen, plump and unassuming in her iron-gray curls, bright cotton dress and flip-flops. Usually Mr. Imwao toured them himself, dressed importantly in his best Philippine-made khakis and island-style shirt, maybe with the mayor in tow. But today, since the visitors were American, Mr. Imwao had grudgingly requested Joyleen's presence. Her American training and fluent English, he thought, might soften them up, and make them more kindly disposed to his appeal for a new operating room. Though he couldn't help finding these international visits intrusive, he was always open to the practice of a little capitalism among friends.

Joyleen stood a little to one side as the group preceded her onto the long ramp leading from the hospital's main entrance to the inpatient wards. Here, louvered windows channeled a welcome cross-breeze that smelled of sea air and rotting vegetation. An elderly woman skirted the edge of the ramp, sopping up rainwater from this morning's downpour with a dank cotton mop.

"This wing," Mr. Imwao explained, "was built two years ago by a team of international volunteers." Joyleen, as she translated, studied the visitors' faces: two men and two women in physicians' lab coats and heavy leather shoes listened with polite attention. A step or two behind them, the new American ambassador and a pair of executives in business clothes pointed out to each other, in stage whispers, the peeling paint, stained ceiling, muddy floors. As if on cue, a scrawny cat emerged from one of the patient wards, and bounded past them down the ramp.

In spite of herself, Joyleen felt a little sorry for the visitors. Damp from the rain and perspiring in their inappropriate clothes, they shifted their heavy laptop bags from shoulder to shoulder, hoping their bravado disguised the discomfort they felt at being surrounded by a culture they didn't understand.

She'd seen the same mix of smugness, curiosity, and dismay on the faces of her own grown children during their rare visits out from their high-tech, high-stress mainland jobs. And it was the same look that had greeted her years ago when she arrived at nursing school in Seattle.

That was back in the 80's, when the Compact of Free Association had been her ticket off the island. With his new U.S. passport, her fiancé had been able to join the U.S. Navy, and she had gladly followed him, away from the long reach and censure of their disapproving clans, away from the dead-ends of subsistence fishing and endless childbearing that had worn down their own parents at an early age. She had been at the top of her class almost in spite of herself; her quiet, self-effacing ways never disguised her competence, just as her exotic appearance had never kept her from good jobs and promotions in the mainland hospitals. But when her husband had died young, his kidneys failing from diabetes, Joyleen had felt the unexpected tug of her island roots, and had returned, dutifully and alone, to give back as best she could.

"Let me take the leaders back to my office," Mr. Imwao was saying smoothly, as the group reached the top of the ramp, "so I can explain more of my plans for the future of this hospital."

He led the ambassador away by the elbow, with the executives, still gesturing and discussing, right behind them. Joyleen smiled at the four doctors, and ushered them into the room from which the cat had just emerged.

"Our chief of staff is here to take you on rounds," she said. She introduced Dr. Jacky, a plump, young man with tired eyes, and then stepped back again to her position of respect.

The group moved slowly among the patients in the ten-bed room, reviewing the details of each one's illness, treatment, and progress. In one bed, a stocky, sullen young man decorated in black tribal tattoos watched wordlessly as Joyleen removed the dressings from a series of deep lacerations that Dr. Jacky had surgically repaired the night before. In another, a pale young man with joints contorted from the ravages of hemophilia awaited a blood transfusion that was being flown in from Saipan, 500 miles away. In a third bed, a woman in her thirties beamed up at them, and obligingly displayed the scar from last week's gallbladder surgery. As they reached the bed in the center of the room, Joyleen slipped behind the woman seated there and placed a protective hand on her shoulder. Kenye, a nineteen year old woman from one of the islands outside the lagoon, sat cross-legged in the center of the rumpled bed, holding an infant. The baby boy wore only a cotton diaper and a ragged lavender blanket decorated with American cartoon ponies. Ill and listless, with every muscle intent on breathing, he lay propped in the crook of his mother's arm.

"This six month-old boy was admitted yesterday afternoon," Dr. Jacky explained, "His x-ray shows pneumonia in three lobes. He has been getting gentamycin, but as you see he is not doing well."

One of the doctors, a young blonde woman, stepped forward and introduced herself to Dr. Jacky as a pediatrician from Philadelphia. Stethoscope in hand, she bent her face close to the pair on the bed.

"How long has your baby been so sick?" she asked Kenye, trying to catch her eye.

Joyleen translated in a soft voice. The young woman shook her head once, and looked away in embarrassment. Undaunted, the pediatrician turned her attention to the baby. She listened carefully to his raspy breathing and briefly stroked his hot dry cheek with the tip of her finger. She stood up and addressed Joyleen.

"He needs oxygen, and fluids. Did he have a chest x-ray this morning? If not, he needs one now."

"Yes, doctor," Joyleen replied, "I will get the x-ray. But he won't take fluids from a bottle, and he isn't nursing."

"IV, then. And the oxygen."

"Yes, doctor. Of course." It seemed shameful to explain that only the TB ward had oxygen, and there were no IVs small enough for this little one's veins. The pediatrician turned to the other doctors with a worried look. "He's tiring out. He's going to need intubation very soon at this rate." They were out of earshot before Joyleen could hear their reply. When the doctors were gone, Kenye looked questioningly up at Joyleen. She spoke no English, and not much of Joyleen's main island dialect.

"The American doctor says they have a treatment. She says your baby will be fine, and you can go home very soon." She held the younger woman's gaze for a moment before Kenye turned her passive face back to her gasping child. Getting no further response, Joyleen sat down on the bed and waited.

Kenye's oversized dress exaggerated how thin she was underneath. Despite her youth, she already wore the patient, faintly sad expression of someone who had already seen too much of life, and no longer expected anything from it. Life on the outer islands, Joyleen knew, was particularly hard. The sandy strips of atoll grew little; the men fished or carved wooden trinkets for the tourist trade. Disease and violence took their toll, particularly on the children;

in the traditional way, babies weren't named until they lived to see their first birthdays. Few grew old out there, beyond the protection of the lagoon.

She took the baby gently, pinching his little thigh to administer the next injection of antibiotic. He screwed up his face to wail but was too weak to make a sound. She comforted him for a moment, then wrapped him in a clean cloth diaper and his blanket, and held him out to his mother.

"Let's try nursing now. He needs to eat to get strong."

Kenye, her eyes downcast, made no move. "Too much child," she said, in a barely audible voice. "No money for sick. Husband no work." She paused for a moment, with a sad, faraway look. "Maybe die better."

Joyleen carried the baby briskly down the hall to the nurse's station, where she dug a small bottle of electrolyte solution from the supply cabinet. Returning to Kenye, she handed her the bottle, and placed the baby gently but firmly in her arms.

"He's thirsty. Please try. If his belly is full, maybe he'll sleep a little."

After the morning rounds, Joyleen escorted the three doctors to the tiny outbuilding that served as the hospital café. They were hailed immediately by two other Americans who had arrived before them.

Joyleen excused herself. "You rest with your friends. I will see you later for afternoon rounds."

Outside, Joyleen waited under the eaves for another tropical downpour to subside. She could see the Americans through the screens as they pulled together two of the sticky tables and collapsed into the plastic chairs with relief, taking in the surroundings. Inside, the power was out again. Lazy flies drifted in the heavy air.

Francis, a tall African-American surgeon, surveyed the menu that was hand-lettered on a piece of cardboard and pinned to the wall. "Mmmm-MMMM," Joyleen heard him joke, "Can't wait to try a local burger."

The Infectious Diseases specialist, a middle-aged Asian-American woman called Sonia pulled a bottle of Japanese-made Gatorade from a tepid cooler. "Please don't eat the raw tuna."

"Fresh off the reef," argued a young optometrist from Chicago.

"This could be an endemic area for the *diphyllobothrium latum* fish tapeworm."

Joyleen felt a sting of pride—local tuna was good enough for the sushi chefs of Tokyo—and then laughed at herself for eavesdropping. The rain stopped for a moment, as suddenly as it had begun. She left the Americans to their lunch and their conversation.

"C'mon now, that tapeworm stuff won't kill you," Francis was saying. "But what about that young guy we saw this morning with those wicked puncture wounds? He is lucky to be alive."

"No kidding," Sonia replied, "Did Dr. Jacky say how it happened?"

"Darts!"

"No way!"

"Yep, made of sharpened rebar, and shot from slingshots."

The pediatrician, Michele, sat back in her chair and rubbed her forehead thoughtfully. "That baby with the pneumonia. I'm really worried about him. Joyleen introduced me to the attending pediatrician after rounds. I tried to explain the situation to her, but she just gave me a lecture about how she'd been here for two years now, a representative of the Cuban government, and she didn't need advice from tourists."

"Ouch!" said Sonia, "Thought we were all here for the same reason? People in need?"

"Well, like I said on rounds, that baby needs intubation, before he tires out." The urgency in Michele's voice rose a notch.

"We're not home, " Sonia cautioned, "There are 500 miles of blue ocean between us and the nearest pediatric ICU."

"But they have a ventilator here. I saw it in a storage room down by the ER."

"In the storage room? Who knows if it even works, or if they have tubes," Francis argued, "Joyleen may be well-trained, but I'll bet she doesn't have nurses qualified to care for that baby 24/7."

Sonia shook her head slowly, "It's a tough situation. Even if he survives this hospitalization, he's not likely to survive once he gets home. I can't imagine what a burden an ill child would be to a family that's barely making it now."

"But we cannot just stand by and let him die. It's our moral and professional duty to do everything we can." Michele stood up, jaw set.

"It's ok, Michele," Francis sighed, and held up his hand. "We're with you. Let's go on back over there and try to do our best for this baby."

Joyleen took the doctors' lunch break as an opportunity to write up her reports for the day. The neat, orderliness of the task usually left her with a sense of productive satisfaction, as though her small corner of the universe was arranged and running smoothly. Today, though, it was no use. Her little lies, first to the American pediatrician, and then to Kenye, left her unsettled and uneasy.

She reached into the shopping bag under her desk and pulled out the weaving she kept with her to work on during lulls. The island grandmothers wove seagrass into baskets and lacy ornaments, adorned with cowrie shells or ivory nut. As a girl, Joyleen had refused to learn the skill from her own grandmother, but now a grandmother herself, she'd felt it was time to learn. She worked for a few minutes, adding a web of knots to the lacy wing of an angel with a cowrie face. Still preoccupied with the American doctors, she tugged at the grass, and it snapped off in her hands.

Joyleen sighed and rose from her chair, rubbing her aching knees. Time to put her dilemmas away and attend to afternoon meds.

The power had not come back on. The ward seemed perfectly still in the heat of the afternoon: patients and families dozed, two or three to a bed, or on the cool floor among plastic bags full of their possessions, their heads propped against the wall. She saw that Kenye and the baby must have gone for the x-ray that the American doctor wanted. Pocketing the syringe containing the baby's next dose of antibiotics, she decided to meet them there.

The x-ray tech was snoring gently behind his desk, chair tilted back precariously on two legs, when she arrived. No, he said, rubbing his bleary eyes, he hadn't seen that baby today. X-ray looked pretty bad yesterday, though. Did she want to see it?

Joyleen declined politely, leaving by a back way that led through to the entry hall, where lines were forming to see the American eye doctor and dentist. No one in the waiting area remembered seeing a young woman with a sick baby. She circled through the muddy courtyard; no Kenye. On impulse, she turned between two outbuildings and down the unpaved road past the boat landing. The twice-weekly boat to the outer lagoon had just pulled away. She tried to spot the girl in the crowd but gave up after a few moments. Patients did this sometimes. They just got tired of the hospital and went home. Sometimes they'd turn up later, sicker. Sometimes they just dealt with whatever they could in their own way. She sighed. This wasn't going to go over well with the blonde pediatrician.

When she returned to the ward, the power was back on. As she walked in, something caught her eye then that had escaped her attention before: the lavender blanket with the cartoon pony design, wadded up at the foot of the now-empty bed. Joyleen scooped up, and then nearly dropped the tightly-wrapped bundle that was much too heavy for an empty blanket. She stood still for a moment, while her rational mind caught up with what her heart already knew.

Kenye had cut her losses. In her world, many babies, too fragile to face the world, die before their naming days. She was young yet. There would always be another baby, perhaps a stronger one to replace the weak. And until then, there were her other little ones. Little ones who need to eat, to grow, who maybe will get by.

Joyleen held the bundle tightly just for a moment, as though she could comfort him, Kenye, herself. But the bundle was unyielding, like the pain in the islanders' hearts, like the suffering of the world. Then she took the little body away.

Returning from the morgue, Joyleen nearly collided with Dr. Jacky, the blonde pediatrician, and the big surgeon striding briskly up the ramp to the ward, pushing a brand-new mechanical ventilator in front of them. An ambu bag, a small plastic mask, and a laryngoscope kit were perched on top. Their pockets bulged with sterile supplies.

"Nurse," he motioned to her, "Give us a hand." Sensing where they were headed, Joyleen scurried to keep up with the three doctors, to explain. They stopped abruptly, parking the instrument next to Kenye's empty bed. Around the room, curious patients raised up on their elbows to look, calling to each other in low voices, gesticulating toward the new machine. Dr. Jacky turned to Joyleen, his head cocked questioningly, eyebrows raised. For the space on one heartbeat, Joyleen's eyes met his. Then she shook her head just once, and stepped back without a word.

"Where's our patient?" Michele, the pediatrician, looked from Dr. Jacky to Joyleen. "Where's the baby?"

The surgeon put a hand on her shoulder and said quietly. "I think we're too late."

She stared at Joyleen for an astonished moment. "Damn it!" she burst out, "Damn this—"

Sensing all eyes on her, she stopped, and swallowed hard. Struggling for self-control, she turned to Dr. Jacky. "That baby could have been saved!"

The room fell silent, stung by her tone, and by the implication of her words. For a long moment, no one spoke, as Michelle continued to stare at the empty bed. Dr. Jacky patted the machine regretfully. Francis, head bowed, studied his shoes. Joyleen looked past them all: the watchful patients, the silent doctors, the ventilator by the rumpled bed. Through the louvered windows, she could see the sun shimmering on the pale turquoise lagoon, where the twice-weekly boat with Kenye aboard slowly made its way toward the white sandy atoll.

"Too much sick," she said, momentarily losing her perfect English, "Maybe die better. God know."

Medea

Jennifer Ruby

It's Medea climbing the stairs,
sights set on the man she loves
and the children she bore.
It's the calculus of nakedness
and of longing.

Shame is lamentation grafted to regret,
An ecology of secrets.

It's the late night peregrinations,
when you imagine that letters in the ceiling,
are an ode to loss.

It's conjecture as faith,
searching the cosmos
for a reason as salve.
Shame is a woman capable
of the worst kind of violence,
It's rocks in her dress pockets
weighing down those narrow stairs.

Map Projection

Jennifer Ruby

What happened to the language of the North?
The language we spoke was
An imperfect translation.
There were no adjectives
to arrest the fall.
No contingencies in the event
Of fire, flood, or marriage.

Instead, I offered this:
A deposition,
The conclusion to Mahler's unfinished
symphony,
The one where he says goodbye.
Drumbeats up through the floorboards,
Blues about exile preserved in a Memphis jukebox.
Borderlands and crossroads
Thresholds painted red,
Strangers exchanging photographs.
A carabiner.
Sisyphus pushing a rock up a mountain.

None of these were my gifts to give,
But I thought you should have them.

In the language map of the world,
You're the route from Finnish to Magyar,
Athabascan to Yuma,
The blue thread of a meridian.

We'll know the way north
by means of
Simply being
The last two speakers
Of a dying tongue.

Begin With a Question

Stacey Johnson

LATELY I GO TO BED EARLY, feigning exhaustion when I am only tired of pretending to take certain things for granted. I need to dream or talk into a pillow. A solitary walk of several months might do it, but that is not an option right now. The heart is running again, tempted to trespass against every fair warning. The last time this happened, I ended up married. Now what?

Love you baby, I say on my way to bed. He sits on the couch, gives a passing glance, and nods. Sometimes I can feel him looking for longer than a glance, when I am walking down the hallway to the bedroom. I think about going back to hold his hand and look earnestly into his eyes and say, Really, really I do. But I do not trust that I can do this without weeping, and when I weep he worries that something is wrong. Which, of course, may be true, but I do not know what, and I certainly do not care to explain. On the rare times that I have attempted to do so in his presence, I have found that this only makes it worse. He will begin speculating that this break is the harbinger of an onset of the mental illness that runs in my family. You need a little blue pill, he will say. Or he will suspect there is someone else, without really being able to imagine all the things that this could mean. I have stopped arguing about such suggestions, and respond mainly with silence and a nod into my book. Or a walk down the hall, into the bedroom. Our apartment is so small that the bedroom is really the only place to go when you want to be alone. The irony of this does not escape me.

I have a sense that the thing that is being borne is something that we can survive, but I do not know how. I mistook him for the strong one—big shoulders, brash way of speaking, the way he was so sure that he was right. I thought that he could hold me down, which was exactly what I needed on account of all the constant questioning I was prone to. This turned out to be true for different reasons than I could recognize at the time.

§

Early to bed, early to rise. Now I am awake with my notebook just after midnight and tomorrow is a Thursday. I have a warm tea bag over one eye, hoping to clear a stye that has become distractingly painful but which is not yet visible unless you look as close as I look when I squint in the mirror in the morning. I have felt it coming on for the past few days, but did not treat it. Now I am worried that it will have obviously erupted by Monday into something that people have to try not to stare at. So now I am on my third tea bag thinking, Please not my face. If I have to appear malformed before the man that has been keeping me awake at midnight and with whom I can never be—except in the world of dreams, we agreed—that would simply be too much.

I have been searching online for an ancient explanation as to the causes of styes, one that offers more than the human-as-machine explanation of bacteria invading a membrane. I come across a few sites of Chinese folk medicine, though I was really looking for classic Greek. It seems to me that the peers of Hippocrates would have had some apt opinion about the cause of this inflammation. There must be some theory about it being rooted in a problem of vision, something about a maladjusted perspective in need of alignment. After an hour of Internet searching, it becomes clear that I will have to go to the library and pore through books if I really want to know, so for now all I have are online versions of traditional Eastern medicine. According to one site, the stye is a problem of the heart. Another points to the liver: too much heat. I suppose that either one would apply in this case.

The last time this happened—not the stye but the other eruption—I was twenty-one or twenty-two. My reading habits made me well aware of the standard explanations and of various names for certain constellations of ailments, and also of prescriptions for treatment. These included: depression and the need for meaningful work, more sleep and less coffee, more social activity, and fewer books. In one book, I came across the word oxytocin, which I learned was the bonding chemical that a mother releases which fuels her fierce attachment to her child. I developed a theory that I might have an excess of this hormone, and indulged in a week or two of feeling sorry for myself on account of my biological imbalance. Still, no relief and only a question. What was it all about?

I try to practice responses in case either one of them asks again, Are you okay? Which the man at work did as we were leaving the Jake's Grill the other day, after he had told the story of his heart's own fluctuations, which he was consistently resisting on account of his marriage. Others had been present at the time, laughing and expounding over beer about life and love, but by the time we were leaving it was only us. He must have seen my eyes grow wet.

How are you doing? he asked in earnest when we stopped in front of our cars.

Fine, of course!

At this, we both laughed and I added, Or not, but either way—

I could not finish this thought though the lump in my throat had been constricting airflow for nearly two hours. That was before we kissed, not so much that it could be called a point of no return, but enough to make sleep impossible afterwards.

By way of treatment, I develop a one-line philosophy that I have been repeating in silence whenever I catch myself entertaining certain lines of thought: A beginning is the surest signal of an eventual end.

As a girl, I used to think that it was only a matter of time before I would meet someone who would sit beneath a tree and read me poetry. It seemed that I had only to grow up into myself somehow, and there I would be, listening. There was no specific poem in mind, but I had always leaned naturally toward the Romantics—Keats, Whitman, Shakespeare—with a special fondness for Blake's mysticism, his undulating bodies reaching between poles of heaven and earth. But poems like this were not the sort that had ever hoped to share with another soul. The poetry that a male stranger would someday read was unknown poetry—not sublime or terribly ground breaking, but thoughtful lines of verse that could be absorbed simply with a sigh, punctuated with the clasping of hands and kiss above the picnic basket beneath the shade of an oak. As a dreamer staring into a ceiling, I had often pictured myself in a Victorian gown of white summer lace, like Anne of Green Gables had worn when she attended University. If you had asked me point blank if I thought it was a little strange for someone to picture their future self in the clothing of a bygone era, I may have said of course. But show me where life works like an answer you once had to a question about what it would be like.

If there is a question at every beginning, I guess for us it was, How do you keep living when it all goes away? We seemed to share a love of driving to campsites where all we had to live on were the items we had loaded into the back of his jeep. We stared at stars and read books in our tents and talked about the things that could not be understood, and of the long roads that had been traveled before we met. I thought about Plato's theory of shared souls

and decided that certain conversations indicated that we had one. He seemed
to agree when he said, It seems like we've known each other before. But it's
been a long time, he added.

Who is this man, I wondered. It was clear that he had several leading roles
within him: warrior, healer, protector, provider. I thought that it was only a
matter of time before one of these took shape.

I should have enlisted, he says from time to time before adding, I thought
about it, you know. Seriously. I should have studied with Maui, he says, of
the teacher he had of sacred fighting arts, who saw the gift of sight in him a
year before he stopped training. I thought it was that he had not been loved
enough, and that over time if I poured what I could give freely into him,
he would see. The man from work reminded me the other day over lunch,
that people do not change; they only become who they are if they have the
strength to face it.

When they let him go from the plant three years ago, and he was so often
wearing an expression of a dog waiting to come inside, I used to tell him,
Look. It gives you time. You can do some of the things you've been wanting
to do. Fish. Read. Walk. Build. Take archery lessons. Start a blog, or a radio
show. The worry that I kept to myself was, It gives you time to think, which is
something that in my experience men do not do well, unless their thought can
be attached to some sort of kinetic energy. My dad used to wax the car on his
day off and the worst thing about having it stolen was watching him look out
the window on Sunday afternoons at a blank space, and wonder, Now what?

The answer for him, was: Survival. Or, as he liked to call it, Preparedness.
He became an enthusiast of all things related to the end of the world. This
was not a new development, only something that had, until the layoff, been
more of a once-every-few-months sort of thing. We used to go through the
emergency bin at the end of every summer on a day when the air was hot and
still and it felt like an earthquake coming.

Do we have water? He would begin as if the question had a precedent.

The right answer was, I'll pick up a few more jugs, just in case.

Lay out the flashlights, he would say. Then he would check each battery,
one by one.

Do you have D's?

Yep. Four.

Waterproof matches?

Here.

Duct Tape?

Here.

We need to be ready, he liked to remind me, in the event of an emergency.

Now the box is a closet even though the space that we live in is one-third the size of what we had before. A need for increased storage space began growing steadily after the layoff, funded by a question I often asked myself about the cost of these supplies as compared to say, an addiction to cocaine or online poker, not to mention treatment for something we could not name.

Now the survival closet is stocked with emergency blankets, waterproof matches, powdered eggs, and bags of water. There are several unopened cases of military-issue MREs, and on the floor and the lowest shelves, the heaviest boxes: ammunition for the .22, the .45, and .16 double-barrel. We need more .22 ammo, he'll remark from time to time. Assorted knives and their requisite sheaths; quick-clot, parachute cord, various first-aid kits, thermal layering systems, and tiny bottles of alcohol, intended for barter, in the event of an economic collapse that renders cash worthless.

I chose to see it as an elaborate call and response poem.

Magnesium fire starter, emergency blankets,

sleeping bags, sleeping mats,

check these for punctures.

Duct tape in case of punctures and for many other reasons. Road flares, compass, map, pocket Bible.

Signal mirror, spare socks, moleskin, iodine,

alcohol, hydrogen peroxide.

Check, check, check.

What if the power went down and we had to use the candles from the emergency supply closet?

We have twenty that will burn for two-hundred hours apiece.

How many nights is four thousand hours?

I heard within this litany other questions that were not said aloud, and my answer seemed to always come down to a deep breath in the dark.

Before we met I used to run. In high school I won a scholarship to a cross-country camp in the mountains of Vermont, and it was there that I met Ed Mathers, a walking legend among long distance runners, then in his seventies. His eyes shone with wet brilliance and he told me that he had been painting watercolors for the last decade. It calmed him, he said, and made him lose track of time the way he used to lose it when he ran. When he spoke he shook terribly with Parkinson's disease, and yet he seemed to radiate stillness. On the last day of camp he gave me a card on which he had painted an ocean, with a pink sky above and the slight strokes of black to indicate birds too distant to name, silhouettes of bodies in flight against the sky. He had taken care with the writing inside, black ink in a slightly shaky hand. The most beautiful things in the world, it read, can not be seen or even touched. This from Helen Keller and she should know because she could not see and had only touch. I carried this around with me for years until one time after moving, I realized that I could not say where it was.

3 a.m. is the cutoff. If I am not back to sleep by then, I begin to get a sense of the kind of day it is going to be. It is 3:05.

I used to hope that my husband would read what I wrote and hear my silence differently. After a few years, I had come to prefer my privacy. Still, sometimes I describe myself in the third person just to be safe. As in, she finds herself consumed with _____. Fill in the blank with any of the deadly sins.

Every three months or so, a portion of one of these pages is blacked out or entirely ripped away. Each voided section is almost always followed by an entry that goes something like this: Of course I did not mean that. It was only my crazy rage, it was only my lack of sleep, my lack of time, my lack of patience, some flare-up of an inherited chemical imbalance. It had nothing to do with him.

On one of those late summer afternoons when the Santa Anas are starting to rise and change on the horizon is a constant theme of every news watch, every hour, he thought that we should begin a notebook. If things went really wrong, the reasoning went, there might be no power. Of course the Internet would be down. He wrote phone numbers, names of family members, medications, and dosages. We added as much of a family tree as either of us could produce, with an intention to flesh out certain branches later.

We should put some recipes in there, he offered.

For what? I hadn't cooked with one in years.

For things you might need to prepare that you're not used to.

My only reply to this was Hmmph, but later when things were really bad, I did some online searching.

I was quite entertained by some of the titles: squirrel fricassee, rat-atoiulle, possum primavera. So now I can tell him, if the time ever comes that we are hungry enough to slaughter rodents, I know what to do with that. I will ask him if sometimes he might bring home live ones so that I can get them drunk.

I have a recipe for grilled rats Bordeaux style, which highlights the subtle flavors of the drunken rats that have been known to populate wine cellars in certain regions of France. Brushed with olive oil and crushed shallots, these are best grilled over a fire of broken wine barrels.

Stewed cane rats, on the other hand, may come home dead because they do not need to be intoxicated. A simple browning in butter and peanut oil is enough to get these going. Then you add tomato, pepper, salt, and enough water to cover the meat. Simmer and serve with rice.

If you are going to use rat in casserole, it is best to braise the meat first. Let it sit in a shallow pan in a bath of butter and white wine at 350 for forty-five minutes or more. This is done immediately after the meat is cleaned in some cases. Some consider this step a vital part of the cleaning process, as it is supposed to mellow the flavors of the meat, making it less musky and close enough to poultry to pass, depending on the flavor profile of the dish.

Once I saw a video of a woman in Tuscaloosa who could dress out six possums in a minute. It's one of those facts that stick in the brain, which has no real relevance to anything else, that the mind returns to again and again like the line of a poem and especially at certain hours. Six possums in a minute, six possums in a minute. There was a steely ferocity in her eyes when she rose to claim her title before any of the men were done. And I wondered if it amazed her to stand there before the crowd with such swift grace, champion of this skill that had become her art.

Now it is almost light and time to address certain things which, taken for granted, are supposed to make a life. I can make coffee, boil eggs, iron a blouse. Now is time to make a list for the grocery store on the way home, and to check the balance so I know if I can use the debit card without another overdraft fee. Before closing, I must remember to do one more thing with these pages. I write, at the top of each, in large capital letters, FICTION, because you never know. One day I could leave one of these notebooks open and his eyes could fall across a page.

What is this, he might wonder. And what is it anyway, but a series of pieces working through the mind like dreams during the time when I should have been sleeping? Memory, fact, fiction, dream: I happen to know that there are lines between these categories, but don't ask me what that knowledge looks like in practice.

I could reply with this: You were right about the notebooks. What will we do when the only thing to eat is something we know nothing about? In the event that vital information goes missing, preserve some other kind of sense. Take nothing for granted. Write it down.

Here they come again, silent and familiar, guarding the dawn.

If you are still listening, what do you hear?

Sibilla Aleramo

Catherine Darby

Instead of Beating Me, My Jealous Husband
seizes them,
all 97 of them,
my flowers, my tongue petals,
my articles of confession,
hostage journals bound and transcribed
my blackened lines, blood
cut from my heart,
he snatches them all, thrusting them
in the fire.

Not satisfied, he ransacks
my Pandora drawers for father's words of compassion,
encouraging letters from editors,
and carries these children across the room
to cast them,
all tongues from my past, crackling,
and with his iron arm,
jabs incessantly
until the last hiss is muted.

Sibilla Aleramo (Rina Faccio), the early twentieth century Italian author shocked Italy in 1906 with her feminist novel, Una Donna.

Washat Wedding

Catherine Darby

Both have sewn their wedding suits
from a single white doe skin
his pants, her dress;
her heart bending over beads
needling for weeks
each bead a separate blessing for marriage,
for all the variations of love,
wide and deep as the Umatilla River.
Marriage here is slow
tradition calls for time to bless each bead.

Wrapped in the nuptial blanket,
they stand on the elk hide,
prayer rug of marriage,
listening to the Wahani elders
naming father and mother of bride and groom
and their fathers and mothers
going back until they cannot speak
because to go back that far calls to silence.
We clap to praise and honor the named and nameless.
They kiss
thundering god drums.
Later when we eat,
an elder woman across from me
stands in prayer
blessing of deer meat, of salmon,
of *camas* sweetening the plate
her left hand on the center of her sacrum

palm facing out
absorbing energy from the earth
right hand on heart
taking in this grounding.

Nuliajuk
Redemptive Analogies and the
Mother of Sea Beasts

David Schmidt

S ETTLE DOWN, CLASS. NOW WHO CAN tell me what a 'redemptive analogy' is?"

The instructor glanced around the circle of students, looking for someone to call on. All the missionaries-in-training stared at each other nervously. The youngest trainee fiddled with his pencil as he stared at the floor. The instructor took this as a clear invitation to call on him. "How about you? I'm sure you could explain the concept to the rest of us."

"I think it's like a legend or myth in a tribe," said the trainee, "that makes them more likely to accept what missionaries teach them. That's what my dad always said, anyway."

"You're on the right track," the instructor replied. "A 'redemptive analogy' is a belief, legend, or tradition in a pagan culture that is similar to the Truth. It opens up a window for us to go and preach the Good News to them. For years now, our missionaries have noticed this phenomenon—in the midst of godless legends and stories, certain concepts exist which foreshadow the Good News."

The discussion had now drawn in the attention of the other students; they all leaned in attentively. One heavy-set trainee chimed in. "I've heard of some Fundamentalists who say that redemptive analogies can't exist. They don't believe there can be any Truth at all in the pagan lies of a tribe's myths."

"I beg to disagree," said the instructor. "Of course, it *is* true that these primitive people are living in darkness. It is true that they need saving. They don't know the joy we have, the peace and eternal happiness we have. That's

---

The legend of Nuliajuk, as told by the Netsilik Eskimo, comes from the book, Northern
Tales: Traditional Stories of Eskimo and Indian Peoples, *by Howard Norman, Pantheon Books,
New York, pages 212-214. Sections of the legend were quoted almost verbatim for the "Scripture
reading" in this story.*

why you are all training for the mission field in the first place. It's why you'll all be heading south in three months—to save souls. But still, I believe that there are nuggets of divine Truth that are hidden in the legends of even the most hopeless, dark tribes on earth."

A female student with plain features and a boyish posture caught the teacher's eye. "Excuse me, Instructor, but don't you think we should open the lesson as we always do—with a Scripture reading? I mean, it is a good way to get off on the right foot."

The instructor wrung his hands. "You're absolutely right, how could I have forgotten? Who wants to lead us in today's Scripture reading?"

The same female student raised her hand to volunteer. She reached behind her, pulled out the parchment printed on seal skin, unrolled it, and cleared her throat. The other missionaries-in-training did the same, opening their seal skin rolls and following as the student read aloud:

"Nuliajuk, the Mother of the Sea Beasts, lives in a house on the bed of the sea. She is quick to anger, terrible in the ways she punishes mankind. She notices every little breach of taboo, she knows everything. Whenever people break a taboo, she hides all the animals; then mankind begins to starve. There are evil spirits that live in the house of Nuliajuk under the sea. If we displease her, she will send the evil spirits out to attack us...."

Piujuq, the female student, continued to read. The missionaries sat through the lengthy Scripture reading, growing increasingly distracted. They had heard these verses quoted so many times, they practically had them committed to memory. The younger members of the group stared up at the roof of the igloo impatiently, pulling their parkas more tightly around their necks.

"...this is all we know of Nuliajuk, the Sea Spirit. She gave us the seals to eat, but she is also full of anger, and sometimes thinks of annihilating us. We must watch our conduct and avoid breaking taboos, so as to not awaken her wrath. Amen."

"Amen," the missionaries-in-training echoed.

"I feel like this is a fitting Scripture reading for our lesson on redemptive analogies," the instructor said as the students rolled their seal skins back up. "Now think back to some of the cultural training you've received thus far.

What elements of the mythology and beliefs of the barbarians to the south could be considered 'redemptive analogies', in light of this Scripture reading?"

For a minute, all was silent inside the igloo. Only the sound of the wind and snow whistling across the smoke hole above, the smell of the warm furs and blankets, the reassuring light from the oil lamp flickering against the icy walls. The students all laid in a circle on the *illeq* floor, their heads toward the center of the circle. They stared around at each other, waiting for someone to speak up.

Finally, the heavy-set student raised his gloved hand. "Well, I remember you telling us that the pagans believed in some sort of sky god of their own, and that he watches people's behavior. That could be a redemptive analogy, couldn't it? I mean, they don't know the Good News about Nuliajuk the Mother of Sea Beasts yet, but this primitive belief of theirs might be paving the way for Her message."

"Excellent, Kalaallisut!" The instructor smiled. "That is a perfect example. The tribes to the South don't know of Nuliajuk by name, but they already have a *concept* in their legends which points to a deity who watches what we do; who is always monitoring our conduct, watching for the slightest breach of any taboo. Our first pioneers who headed south and studied these tribes discovered that there is a whole complex series of legends about how quick to anger their 'sky god' is. This is an inroad for the Good News—it's a redemptive analogy that has prepared their minds for the message of Nuliajuk!"

The missionary students hummed together, muttering "*e'en*" in affirmation.

"I think it's a real blessing that the pagans are ready for the Gospel of Nuliajuk," said Piujuq, reaching for a second fur pelt to wrap around her neck. "I remember one of our textbooks said that they believe that if they defy their god's rules—if they drink alcohol, or listen to forbidden music, or have sexual feelings that go against his taboos—they might be attacked by evil spirits. It's sad that they live in fear like that. They don't know the joy of having faith in Nuliajuk."

"That's why Nuliajuk has prepared them to hear the Good News," the instructor responded, adding more seal oil to the lamp. "Despite how far away the pagans of the south live. They've never had missionaries go to preach the Good News of the Sea Spirit to them yet, but Nuliajuk has set eternity in their hearts."

A wiry male student with longer hair than the rest raised his hand. "So does this mean the pagans have a redemptive analogy for every holy doctrine of Nuliajuk? I mean, do they have any sort of mythical Creation Story that is similar to the truth—how the Sea Spirit cut her fingers off and transformed them into seals?"

"Unfortunately, no," the instructor responded, edging closer to the fire in the center of the circle. "Not as such. The pagans don't know about Nuliajuk cutting her fingers off yet. Their Creation Story is very backwards and convoluted—it involves talking snakes and apples and naked people made from dirt. But you don't need to worry about that for now. When you first head out into the mission field, your primary concern should be getting people saved. Bring them to faith in the Mother of the Sea Beasts; help them cultivate a personal relationship with Nuliajuk."

Kalaallisut finished chewing a large piece of whale fat he had stuffed into his mouth, and spoke up. "It's like we studied in 'Principles of Eskimo Missiology 101.' You focus on the basics of the Good News first. Help them realize that Nuliajuk is always watching what we do, teach them to fear Her, make them aware that she retaliates quickly and fiercely when we offend her. Teach them the Scriptural truth—that Nuliajuk will hide all the game animals from us if we break Her taboos. Everything else is secondary."

"Absolutely right, Kalaallisut," said the instructor. "Eventually, with patience, you can teach the pagans the true Creation Story. Bit by bit, you can correct their mythology, bring them to a knowledge of the Truth, explain about Nuliajuk's fingers transforming into seals, and they'll reject that nonsense about the snake and dirt people and apples on their own."

The youngest trainee still sat at the back of the igloo, staring intently at the furs and pelts beneath him. The instructor addressed him. "What about you, Ujarak? You seem awfully quiet today."

"It's just that... it's nothing, sir."

"Come on, out with it, Ujarak. There's no such thing as a stupid question."

"Well I was just thinking... we say we're bringing hope and light to these people, that the Word of Nuliajuk is 'the Good News.' Right?"

The igloo had grown quiet. The students had stopped humming "e'en," not sure where Ujarak was going with his question.

"But every now and then I get to thinking... what is so good about it? I mean, they're afraid of their sky god punishing them, they're afraid they'll get attacked by demons if they disobey him. They are always walking on eggshells trying to not step out of line, or else he might send them to this 'fire under the earth' that they believe in. Primitive, right?"

The other students nodded cautiously.

"But what's so different between their pagan beliefs and our 'Good News'?" Ujarak continued. "We're just as afraid of Nuliajuk as they are of their sky god. We're basically just asking them to trade in one set of fears for another. We tell them not to fear their sky god's fire under the earth, but then we just tell them they should fear all of Nuliajuk's terrifying servants instead: Her Black Guard Dog, Her companions like Isarrataitsoq, 'The One with No Arms,' Ungaq 'The One Who Screams.' How is that a real alternative to the 'darkness' they live in?"

The circle of missionaries-in-training stared at Ujarak in silence. The fire crackled. The icy wind blew outside the igloo. Somewhere in the distance, a wolf howled.

"I want to see you in my igloo after class," the instructor told Ujarak sternly. "I think it might be time for you to rededicate your life to Nuliajuk."

The Horror of that War

Nancy Sandweiss

tears through me once again. Astride a stationary bike, I feel the heat
of battle, earphones a conduit to my heart. As I listen to a novel
about Viet Nam, festering memories erupt. Mangled bodies,

burned out villages, broken soldiers—indelible images from college
years. These days I hear echoes of that hell in the blast of roadside bombs,
drone of unmanned aircraft, bombastic politicians. But here in the gym,

tv screens feature celebrity cooks, grinning talk show hosts, gridiron
heroes. Iraq, Afghanistan, are intermittent static, not staples
of the evening news. Untouched by combat, few of us know sacrifice...

Leaving the gym, emotions bruised, I pass a woman, who chirps,
Are you connected with the military? Her display table features baby
clothes—sleepers, rompers, bibs—in camouflage print.

Eyes downcast, I shake my head. An old song jumps to mind:
I didn't raise my son to be a soldier.

Monarch Butterflies

Christian Benavides

To fight was to survive,
my dad once told me.
In his village, he said every kid
kept his hand in a fist.
And every kid kept dreams of
big cities balled up at
the edges of their eyes.
One day, he spread my hands
wide open,

> *You're a butterfly, mijo,*
> *on your back, you carry*
> *lifelines of past generations,*
> *all buried in unmarked graves*
> *but breathing through you.*

And in his words, cracked
and peeling,
I heard the echoes of thousands
like me.
All kids who kept their hands
in a fist.
But all whose arms now fluttered high
in the air.
I was part of those who made it to the
golden nectar.

Live, whispered the wind beneath us,
and you'll live for us too.

Her Mother's Glasses

Niki Shaffer

W HEN AMANDA SAW HER MOTHER'S PHONE number pop up on her caller ID screen that morning, she resolved to let the call roll over to voice mail. But then her office cubicle mate, Carmen, told her to pick up because the ringing was driving her crazy. Amanda snatched up the receiver. "Hi, Mom," she said, "What's wrong now?"

"Oh, hello, darling," her mother, Ruth, said. "How did you know it was me?"

"Mom. I've told you a million times I have caller ID on my work phone. What do you want?"

"Why do you even need to know who is calling? Isn't that illegal in some way?"

"No, Mom, it's not illegal," Amanda said. "Tell me what you want."

"Well," Ruth said, "I have no idea how such a thing could even be possible. It's all over my head."

"Mom. I am busy. I am going to hang up now," Amanda said.

"Oh, well," her mother said. "I am very sorry to intrude on your busy life, with your spy phone and all. I wanted to tell you that I can't find my green glasses."

"Mom, go look for them," Amanda said. "Don't call me at work to tell me you can't find your glasses, for God's sake."

"I am calling you to report a theft," Ruth replied with some dignity. "I believe that cleaning lady you hired stole my glasses."

"Mom, that is ridiculous," Amanda said. "Lucy did not steal your glasses. Nobody on God's earth would even want those hideous green Mrs. Magoo things."

"Well, you needn't be insulting, Amanda. I, for one, love my 'hideous' green glasses," Ruth said. "Lucy has complimented me on them before. I could tell she coveted them. That is why she stole them. She's probably wearing them south of the border right now."

"If she is, she's the laughing stock of Tijuana," Amanda said. "Look, Mom, I have to go. Just wear your spare pair. I'll come over later and find your green glasses then. They're probably sitting right on top of your head."

"No, they are not, Miss Smarty Pants," Amanda's mother said. "I already checked there."

"Well, good, Mom. I'll see you around 5:30. I am going to say good-bye now. Don't call me back anymore, okay?"

"But what if it's an emergency?" Ruth asked.

"Then call 911. Good-bye, Mom." Amanda resisted the impulse to slam down the receiver as she hung up the phone.

A few minutes later, Carmen knocked on the shaky pseudo-wall of their shared office cubicle. Amanda and Carmen worked in a high rise office building in downtown San Diego where the windows were tinted and permanently sealed. Lacking any other source of stimulation besides the dull legal work they were paid to do, they often sought each other out for conversation. Carmen was one of the few people in Amanda's office who was actually older than Amanda, though both were middle-aged. Their shared "cubicle hell" existence had rendered any expectation of privacy obsolete long ago. Carmen asked, "More drama with Mama?"

"Same old stupid stuff," Amanda said. "Now she thinks the cleaning lady stole her glasses."

"Well," Carmen said, "maybe she did."

"Carmen, that's crazy. Don't take her side."

"Amanda, you forget. I am a mom myself, who misses her own mother dearly. I am always on the side of moms. Especially the older they get," Carmen replied. "Amanda, you need to remember we only get one mother in this life."

"Yeah, well thank God for that," Amanda said. "My one and only mom will outlive us all. But, thanks, Carmen. I need to finish this report so I can leave on time and deal with the great stolen glasses caper."

Later that afternoon, Amanda took the elevator down to the parking garage in her building, which resembled nothing more than a concrete prison. She had not seen the sky or breathed in any fresh air since early that morning. No time for that now. Her mother's missing glasses must be dealt with, as asinine of a chore as ever there was. Amanda searched through her old Saturn's front passenger seat on the off-chance her mother's glasses had fallen somewhere the last time Amanda had taken her to a doctor's appointment.

Amanda found several items of certifiable old lady debris that her mother had left behind. Here a half-used cough drop, carefully replaced in its original mint green wrapping; there, some shredded pale green tissue paper the color of old lettuce. Amanda's mother's favorite color had always been green, with a strong preference for the chartreuse end of the spectrum, and she was inclined to purchase any conceivable item in that shade whenever possible. Amanda picked through the assorted green debris, and, finding no glasses, started up her car and drove off to her mother's apartment.

Amanda's mom lived in a condominium building near the ocean, which was ironic, since most of its occupants were too old and infirm to enjoy the beach ever again. Although it was not a strict requirement that people who resided in this building be elderly widows, such a policy appeared to be enforced by self-selection of the residents. Amanda parked in one of the few visitor spots that was not reserved for the handicapped. She waved to a couple of old ladies who seemed to be trying to catch her attention and hurried up the stairwell where they could not follow.

The Land that Time Forgot, Amanda thought as she walked down the hall to her mom's apartment. She smelled liver and onions frying; who actually ate that stuff anymore? She could hear the bleat of multiple television sets, calling out "Wheel of Fortune," and "Judge Judy," favorites of her mother's fellow residents. Amanda pictured a sea of old ladies, huddled over their TV trays, eagerly waiting for the local news so they could be sure not to miss the weather report. As if they ever go outside anyway, Amanda thought. Many of these ladies shared a crush on Tom Bollman, the still dapper elderly weatherman on one of the local stations. "His wife's a lucky woman," one of them told her last month. "Get a life," Amanda thought.

As Amanda came to the end of the hallway where her mom lived, she could hear the sound of her mother singing, something from, "My Fair Lady." Amanda paused outside her mother's door, remembering the many times her mother had sung her to sleep when she was a child, in such a loving sweet voice. Everyone had remarked on Ruth's beautiful singing voice when Amanda was young. But now, her mother's voice had lost much of its luster and range. She could no longer hit most of the notes, and Amanda's mom just sounded creaky and old.

Amanda sighed, and knocked several times. But her mom could not hear her, or much of anything else, these days. Amanda used her key, interrupting her mother's rusty rendition of "I'm Getting Married in the Morning." "Hi, Mom," Amanda said. "Bad news, Tom Bollman is already married."

"Oh, Amanda, you scared me," her mom said. "I wasn't expecting you. And who is Tom Bollman?" Amanda saw right away that her mom was wearing the allegedly stolen green glasses, in addition to her ever present lime green cardigan. Even though it was mid-July, it seemed Amanda's mother was always cold these days.

"Mom. What do you mean you weren't expecting me? You called me at work to say you couldn't find your glasses. You were sure Lucy had stolen them," Amanda said. Amanda's mother was trying without much success to lift herself off the couch. The couch was the same one that had been in Amanda's parents' house when she was growing up. It was green, of course, a darker shade of green, like spinach, and was sprinkled with a floral pattern consisting of small flowers of varying shades of green found nowhere in nature. Amanda walked over to the couch and bent down, using both of her arms to help pull her mother up off her childhood couch.

"Oh, that's right," her mother said. "You did tell me you were coming. Well, I found my glasses in the night stand right after I spoke to you. But it is always so lovely to see you, darling." Amanda's mom hugged her daughter and rested her head on Amanda's arm for a second. Her mother seemed to be shrinking, Amanda thought. Wasn't it just last year her mom's head had reached her shoulder? Amanda remembered all of the pencil markings her parents made on the wall keeping track of their daughter's height while she was growing up. Maybe there should be a reverse set of marks for when we grow old, Amanda thought, although she did not share this insight with her mother.

"Mom. Why didn't you call me back to tell me you found your stupid glasses? I left work early just to come rushing over here for no reason," Amanda said.

"But you scolded me," Amanda's mother said. "You told me not to call you back unless it was an emergency."

"Oh, well. All right, Mom. I am glad you found your glasses. Do you have anything else you need as long as I'm here?"

"Well, I still think that woman you hired is stealing from me. I will be counting my change before you bring her back next time," Amanda's mother said. "But, I don't need anything right this minute. Can't you stay for supper, honey? I have some of that soup you like from Falcone's. And then we can watch the news together."

"No, Mom. I haven't even been home yet, and now I've already wasted time for nothing over here," Amanda said.

"I am sorry you feel that way," her mother said. "It is never a 'waste of time' to visit your mother, Amanda."

"No, no, Mom, of course not. But, I do have to go. I will see you on Thursday when we go see Dr. Wallace," Amanda said, now itching to leave.

"All right, honey. Will you have time for lunch then?"

"Probably not," Amanda said, as her mother shuffled along with her to the door. "But, we'll see. Bye, Mom. Hold onto your glasses."

"Oh, good-bye, darling. I wish you could stay," Amanda's mother said.

"Me, too," Amanda lied. "See you soon."

As she practically rushed down the hall, Amanda heard her Mom call, "I love you." "I love you, too," Amanda said, though she knew her mother couldn't hear her anymore.

On her way back to her car, Amanda was unable to avoid a conversation with Mrs. Corbin, her Mom's second floor neighbor. Mrs. Corbin, who looked to be approximately the age of Methuselah, had recently acquired a Jazzie, which enabled her to ensnare most visitors in her path, so as not to be run over.

"Amanda," Mrs. Corbin said. "I thought that was you. Have you been to see your mother? How is she?"

"Hi, Mrs. Corbin," Amanda said, resigned to her fate. "Mom is fine. I am just on my way home."

"Well, I am glad to hear that," Mrs. Corbin said. "Ruth has seemed a bit frail lately."

Amanda thought, "At least she's not in a flippin Jazzie." Out loud, she said, "No, she's fine, Mrs. Corbin. We're going to see her doctor later this week to make sure."

"That's good," Mrs. Corbin said. "I still miss my own mother. She was always my best friend. Well, besides Jesus, that is. Anyway, you should take good care of your mother while you still have her with you."

"Okay, I will Mrs. Corbin," Amanda said, sneaking her way around the Jazzie. "Have a good night."

"You will be glad you did after your mother dies," Mrs. Corbin said, but Amanda did not turn around. She thought, "Why don't you go tell your best friend all about it?" Amanda fully expected her mother to live forever.

She didn't, though, of course. Defying all Amanda's expectations, though no one else's, Amanda's mother eventually died. After she did, Amanda had time to think about how much she would like to go have supper with her Mom, maybe watch the evening news together. But, no matter how often Amanda looked at her caller ID screen, it remained stubbornly dark.

A year or so later, Amanda learned she now needed glasses. She took her prescription to a store featuring wall to wall frames on display. The salesperson brought several pairs for Amanda to try, but she found she didn't care for any of them. Something she remembered caught her eye in the very lowest row of the display case. Amanda started walking toward the familiar sight.

"It looks like something special has caught your eye," the salesperson said, hurrying after her so as not to lose his sale.

"Yes, it has," Amanda said. "I'd like to try on the green ones, please."

Rear View Mirror

Rebecca Chamaa

When your mind tilted
a different way on its axis,
you cooled your bacon in a glass
of orange juice, added creamer
to your Coca Cola, and kept raisins
in your shirt pockets to snack on.
I often found them stuffed between
the pillows on the oversized chair
where you sat happily for hours
staring out the window at, I don't know,
memories older than me?
Than my mother? As a young girl,
you went to college and had dreams.
Maybe you found them outside
that window in your final days
as cars passed down the street
with drivers heading for their destinations...

I Can See That

Anthony Conwright

I T STARTED WITH GRAPES. GRAPE STARTED with a chat with Ms. Serena Blue about the modern LGBT movement, the flaccid backbone of the American Liberal Party, and modern chick lit. I dropped the names of a few British poets (American women become soppy at even the thought of British accents), gave my best Hemingway reading, and untethered a feigned blasé flick of the wrist to procure the wine. I did not plan to have the taste of yesterday, however sweet, on my tongue today, but I woke up this morning and discovered myself in my room lying next to a sleeping Serena Blue.

The room wasn't spinning, but it did feel alive. The smell of grape from the evening before was still lingering on the breath of the walls. The floor was haggard with a few bottles of wine, my favorite dinner jacket, a black dress, shoes, and heels. The bed was suffused with the naked bodies of Serena, our intimacy, and me. Serena had her share of cracks, blotches, and cellulite, but all of it together with the curve of her lower lip that slightly protruded her upper one, made her meet the prerequisites of my bedding. Not that my bed is that picky; I'm permitted to sleep in it.

I wanted water, but the rounds of her shoulders, where her perfectly fed and swarthy colored hair meets her collarbone, were still on my lips. I would have ventured off into my tiny kitchen if it weren't for Serena opening her eyes. Watching a beautiful woman sleep is almost as fulfilling as watching that same woman wake up. Her sleep was demure. She couldn't help but be beautiful even when she was sleeping. Her attractiveness never took time off. At the moment her eyelashes unveiled her pupils, I placed my palm on the side of her cheek.

"So, this isn't *just* going to be drunken sex if we keep going," she said. She did not want to think about the consequences of having "sober-sex." Sober-sex means sex with clarity, sex with intention, and without excuse. To blame *this*, or our little affair, on alcohol is one thing, but to blame it on liking each other is something else.

"You didn't want to have sex?"

"No. I did, but I didn't want to follow through..."

"Why didn't you say something?"

"I was going to go into my room, but when you kissed me, I knew that I would have sex with you. You're fun to kiss."

I was worried about my kissing. I've *always* been worried about my kissing. My lips are larger than most and I have a phobia of bad smell, particularly when it is coming from me. We were embarrassingly rich in kisses last night. Kisses on the floor, kisses on hands, kisses clothed, and kisses unclothed.

"So, if I want to have sex with you, I just need to start making out with you?"

"No. I mean... I do want to have sex, but if I have sex with you again, I'm going to want to have sex with you all the time, and that's exactly the problem. I *have* to see you everyday."

"Does that mean you can't look at me without thinking about having sex with me?" I served the question with a hint of sarcasm and a smile, hoping to receive some sort of validation.

"Don't you think it would be weird? To sleep with your roommate?"

"It only makes sense to sleep with someone you are living with. The real issue is when you aren't having sex with the person you are living with." Serena didn't know I knew she and her beau, Tim, were temporarily abstinent. The locus of their issue was Serena's wanting to live with him and to marry, but Tim was in quasi "bachelorhoodum." They were working out the chastity in their relationship, but their solidarity did not deter my moral compass. I seemed to be able to navigate my way through having sex with a "taken" woman.

Sex with Serena wasn't weird at all. It did not take long for our bodies to become acquainted. She touched well and with purpose. She wrapped her arms around my back to pull me close and catch her rhythm. We breathed together, moved together, and she wiped the droplets of sweat from my face like a mother would tears. There were aspects of our sex, however, that could have been more gracious. Dressing myself in the condom was one of the more ungainly tasks. Trying not to notice myself roll lubricated rubber up my skin felt like trying on a suit in a department store. My father taught me every man should own a good suit and wear it well. Putting on a good suit is not like dressing in leisure jeans and a tee shirt. Effortlessly sliding the arms down and out the sleeve and tugging the collar of the suit jacket for the perfect fit around the chest and shoulders is an art. It's especially unattractive for a man to lack the ability to wear a suit and walk in one.

"I can see how it would be a little weird, but I'm not worried about it," I answered.

"And I don't want to like you," Serena cathartically confessed.

"I can see that."

"But I do want to have sex with you."

"I can see that." 'I can see that' was my stock reply when I was hearing someone, but not listening or at least not caring. It was the same type of stock reply my father would give me every time I asked a series of nonsensical questions, to which he replied in spates of indolent "yeah's." Ostensibly, sober-sex is sex that will lead to feeling. It is sex that does not trespass on inhibitions. For Serena, sober-sex could mean the end.

"How are you going to feel when Tim comes over?" She asked as if I had to feel something.

"I'll be fine. What happens in your relationship isn't my business. But I'm not going to say anything, if that is what you are asking." But of course I will say something. Not to Tim, though. Not to the Adonis reincarnate—doctoral candidate in education, Tim. Not the Tim whose words are only slightly less attractive than his voice. Serena will talk about it, but not with Tim. Not with her boyfriend of two years. Not with the man she wants to like. But, she will talk. All women talk. In the world of mass loquacity, someone will talk. Some evidence will surface: a tweet, Facebook post, or a conversation alluding to the bond Serena and I have developed over the last six months. Someone will be privy to my insecurities that manifested themselves during sex. Someone will know about the way I forged passion in my hands to touch Serena. Someone will know I was afraid to make eye contact because she would see that I already *did* like her. Someone will know that, to Serena, I am a fleeting thought.

The doorbell rings. It's Tim. Serena and I were in bed latched onto each other. A legs wrapped around here, a leg wrapped around here, a leg wrapped around there, my hand on her waist, and arm around her shoulder. There is a knock on the door. It's Tim. We roll out of bed and tidy up the secret in my room. Serena greets Tim at the door. Their kiss, in public, is not what our private ones just were. Their kiss looked stale and antiquated. He flopped on the couch noticing the weather on my face.

"Long night John? You look as if you're dying."

My hangover was dying. My grape was dying. Liking Serena was a worthless commodity like having children too soon. When your feelings need pampering the heart will beat, kick, and piss feeling from your eyes and if you're lucky enough you've recently cried, so the acidity of tears won't hurt as much.

I looked over at Tim and once back at Serena realizing why Serena will not like me and why we will not have sober-sex and replied to Tim, "I can see that."

Lost at Sea?

Jill G. Hall

Hubcap in the sky,
a summer silver sun,
sinks beyond the horizon.

Mist rolls in,
paints the beach
with a clear coat of dew
and the roar of invisible waves.

It's time to go
but even so
I watch and wait
on the sandy shore
for the Opanui to return from the open sea.

My heart worries you've been lost.

Crashed and tussled
over roiling waves
of seaweed and dark tar.

The wind picks up,
a foghorn bleats
like a moaning ghost.

Our love has run amok
or at least been stranded
in a giant ocean of lost desires.

Blue Door

Judith Hansen

In Morocco, she's drawn to a structure and snaps a photo. Is it
   a house, a mosque, a tomb? The door is painted blue and
   keyhole-shaped. A square gold border surrounds it. Stone
   steps

leading up to the door are softened by moss and tangled grass,
   a deep cool green. The walls, painted white long ago, are
   cracked, its corners blackened; yet it stands composed

in the delicate ground cover, half in the shadow of a large but
   anonymous tree. She would like to live here for a week, a
   month, maybe more. Sit on the steps and write in a notebook,
   sweet

tea at her elbow. She imagines how satisfying the simplicity of
   this act would be of sitting on the steps, writing, in the cool
   sunshine. No one disturbs her, no flies land in her tea cup.

(She knows that, for her, the practice of writing is ill-fitted and
   uncomfortable. It scratches like wool on a bare neck, or slides
   around her wrists and fingers like clunky costume jewelry.)

This is a gentle vision (and one of many) she has of herself, writing,
   in certain spots all over the world; this person that she is,
   engaged in the simple act of writing—straightforward,

guileless, exposed—is still undiscovered, beyond the blue door,
   which at any moment might creak open, allowing a narrow
   shaft of light within its naked walls.

Smack Down

Terri Dugan

THE SIDEWALK AND PAVEMENT WERE WET with rain. EMT's pushed the gurney carrying Gaston through the double doors and down the hall. Cordelia sat in her car at the far end of the hospital parking lot looking at the red letters spelling Emergency.

She began to cry. She thought Gaston had been coping, holding on to the world and springing back to himself. But lately incidents began to pile up.

One Sunday he called the minister's wife *The Freakin' Countess of Bathory,* the next Sunday referring to her as *My deep fried cream filled delight.* When an aged man shuffling with a walker passed him in the supermarket snack aisle, Gaston said to him, "Any time you pull your head out of your ass, please stop by for a popsicle." It was a month since he Reddi-Wipped his dog, dotting him with maraschino cherries.

Gaston was doing better. He recognized his wife and toothbrush every day; his children and barbecue grill most days. Lately, Gaston had been threatening, but never violent. But, today's altercation snapped off his tether and like a tightly coiled main spring, he was unwinding, coming undone and drifting away from his big life, and away from Cordelia.

Today Gaston was with his family at The Lobster Shack, sitting, laughing, stuffing themselves, living it up. Then a waiter came by with a load of cornbread muffins. It may have been the tongs that set Gaston off. He sprung at the young man, administered a quick Mongolian Chop, then drop kicked him onto the buffet table. The guy was out cold.

Gaston collected himself quickly. "Now, what have I done?" he said.

The waiter was curled around the potato salad, his shirt soiled with remoulade and butter sauce, his feet displacing the hush puppies. He whimpered softly.

By the time the ambulance came, the waiter was coming around. He wasn't off the buffet table but managed to loosen his own collar and curl himself into a fetal position. When his manager came by to check on him, he was able to express doubt about coming in the following day. When fellow wait staffer Dina put a hand on his arm, he looked to her with glassy eyes and told her sincerely that working with her had been the high point of his life. He encouraged her to remember him forever.

Gaston was remorseful yet lucid when questioned by the EMT. Unable to recall any of the incident, he reported that his tongue felt tingly. A second ambulance was dispatched to carry Gaston to hospital for further evaluation. Outside the ER, Cordelia fished into a used fast food bag. She pulled out a ketchup-stained napkin and honked her nose into it. That was one of the things Gaston said he loved about her. He said she sounded like a wild animal when she blew her nose.

Cordelia wanted to go in, to sweep past the waiting room where dozens were doomed to a night of endless waiting, to walk past the desk, and glide over the glossy waxed linoleum. She wanted to go into the bowels of the emergency room where life hurried and abated. She wanted to fling back the suspended curtain of Gaston's cubicle and wrap her arms around his big neck.

But she wouldn't go in. Cordelia was not a part of Gaston's family life. She was unknown to all of them but his brother Ellis. It was Ellis that called her as he followed behind Gaston's family car, which followed behind the ambulance. Gaston kept his life in neat boxes that lined up together but didn't touch.

In one happy, intense, and lucrative box, he had his wrestling; the performances, the workouts, the promotional appearances.

He kept his family together in another box. They were sloppy and sprawling, mostly wrestlers, all loud and open to aggressive suggestion. There was his wife Debbie, his daughters Mimi and Magda the Sleeper, and his son Ambergris the Annilator.

When he was with them, he embraced them like a mad, zany, loving bear-man just the way he embraced Cordelia when he was with her.

There was another box, a tight little perfumed one with a dusky pink ribbon. This is where he kept his women; the wrestling groupies, the infatuated assistants, two waitresses at Steak King, the Assistant Manager at King's Tile and Stone. This is where he kept Cordelia.

Cordelia knew about the other women. She'd resigned herself years ago to the fact of them, which was simply that they occupied Gaston for a time, for an hour or for a season. He loved them and he would be with them for as long as he was with them.

She was used to it. She endured, waited her turn, which always came, had come for the last seven years. It wasn't that Gaston loved her less, but he didn't love them less. Gaston had a big heart and loved everybody.

Years ago, before Cordelia knew better, before she knew that Gaston was born to love the world equally yet separately, she tried to force a reckoning on him. She loved him best, and she wanted him to put her above the others.

She stalked him with his other loves.

One time, she went to Steak King, hung out, and ordered a KC sirloin. Gaston was there. Cordelia sat eyeing him as he sat in his red upholstered booth, eating a rare t-bone blanketed in catsup, watching the legs of the waitress. Cordelia checked out the waitress's legs. They were OK. Decent if you liked well developed calves as Gaston did, the kind of calves that would be good pulling a Rolling Thunder on an opponent. Whatever. Cordelia tried to keep her legs up, going to aerobics on Tuesday and Thursdays.

Gaston smiled and waved when he saw Cordelia. God help him, he didn't have a clue. He just sat there chewing with his mouth open, grinning.

As Gaston finished his meal, the waitress showed up wearing a coat, and the two of them walked right by Cordelia's table.

"Hi hon, it's so great to see you," Gaston said. He was holding the waitress's hand. "What cha doin' here?"

Cordelia's face was burning. "Oh, just getting a bite."

"Enjoy your meal, sweetheart," Gaston leaned in and gave Cordelia a quick catsupy smack on the lips. "Great to see you."

Another time Cordelia went to King's Tile and Stone and sat down with the assistant manager. Her name was Cindy, and Cordelia knew that she was one of Gaston's women. Cordelia didn't reveal her relationship with Gaston to Cindy. She told her that she was remodeling her bathroom and gave her the square footage.

Cordelia wound up liking Cindy. She was still driving around with a trunk-load of porcelain tile that looked like stone yet was easy to install and virtually care-free to maintain.

During the times when Cordelia intersected with another part of Gaston's life, he had no idea that she was trying to gather information about this aspect or that woman and that she wanted to usurp his current attention to herself.

He was always authentically happy to see her, like something serendipitous had occurred. He greeted her, hugged her, sometimes kissed her, then went back to his engagement. He never invited her to join in and he never seemed to be uncomfortable even when everyone else was.

Cordelia stopped stalking around Gaston's other life after a couple of run-ins with his wife Donna, who was his wife before Debbie, but came after his wives Lola and Felice.

Donna was a wrestler that went by the name Donatella, Darling of Darkness.

At one of Gaston's bouts, Cordelia was sitting in the eighth row. Donna was sitting in the second. At some point in the match, as Gaston climbed up onto the ropes, he spotted Cordelia in the audience. He smiled, waved, then jumped off and gave Majick Martin a flying elbow smash in the throat. Majick went down, Donna came up, turned around to see who Gaston was waving at. Her eyes met Cordelia's and she knew that Cordelia was more than a spectator to Gaston. The next day Donna came into Cordelia's work with her arms full of phone books. She stood in the lobby and tore all the phonebooks in half with her bare hands, then clapped those hands together three times and left.

The following Sunday, Donna was waiting next to Cordelia's car when Cordelia came out of church. Donna bent over and grabbed under the frame of the car and lifted until the tires were ten inches off the ground. She let the car drop, pointed at Cordelia and walked off.

Donna was tragically suffocated during a pre-match nap when Snake Queen Rita's python slithered into her dressing room and swallowed her head and upper torso. Cordelia hoped she'd be the next Mrs. Gaston. But Gaston married Debbie. After that, Cordelia stopped trying to garner more of Gaston's attention and vowed to enjoy the time she spent with him.

And the time she spent with him was good, and it was rare lately that he seemed confused or angry or out of touch with reality.

Then came today and the Lobster Shack incident.

Afterwards, Gaston's brother Ellis called Cordelia to let her know what was going on. Ellis called the women that he thought would want to know about Gaston. Since Cordelia was near the start of the alphabet, she was notified early and was the first to arrive at the hospital.

She thought more about going inside. She wasn't family but this was a public place. For anyone concerned, she could be going in to see an ailing friend. If she went inside, she may get a glimpse of Gaston. Besides that, she needed to pee.

Cordelia could wait no longer. She wanted to see Gaston, and she was eager to use the bathroom. As soon as she made up her mind and got out of the car, she looked up to see Gaston's daughter, Mimi, come outside for a smoke. Mimi wasn't a wrestler but she'd killed two men and a municipal bus with her bare hands. She made her deceased stepmother Donna look sane. "Crap," said Cordelia.

Instead of continuing inside, instead of getting back in the car, Cordelia opened up the back driver's side door and, trying to be inconspicuous, she pulled down her underwear, hiked up her skirt, squatted between the two doors, and peed onto the pavement.

Cordelia was concentrating, trying to avoid wetting her shoes when she became aware of a hulking presence. She saw the feet first, a man's size 14. It could only be Gaston's brother Ellis. She didn't look up. She didn't say anything, just pulled up her underwear, threw down her skirts, climbed into the back seat, and curled up.

Ellis closed the back door then hunched his six foot six frame into the driver's seat.

Cordelia was finished crying, exhausted by it. She fell into a deep sleep as he drove through the night.

Ellis pulled into Cordelia's darkened driveway and cut the engine. He went to the back seat, gathered her into his arms, and carried her up the steps to her house.

He lay Cordelia gently on the bed and switched on the bedside lamp. He pulled off her shoes and placed them neatly under the bed. He reached under her, unzipped her skirt, and tugged it down. He gently draped it over a chair. She was awake now and watching as he leaned in and began unbuttoning her blouse. Ellis froze.

Her eyes were liquid, her cheeks stained from crying. He started to tear up just looking at her sad, exhausted face. Patting her back, he planted a soft kiss on the top of her head. She took his hand and began helping him with her blouse. She stretched up and kissed him on the lips.

Where Gaston was all deep musk, Ellis smelled fresh, powdery, like he'd just showered with deodorant soap. Gaston was bear-like and roundish, his stomach, back, and shoulders covered with thick dark hair. Ellis was angular, taller, leaner with a fine sandy hair coiled on his chest and down his abdomen. Both were strong, large men, but Gaston gratified himself, hungrily, aggressively, and quick in movement. Ellis was slow, liquid, languid. Ellis wrapped Cordelia up, pulling her into lovemaking.

Cordelia slept deeply, dreaming of Gaston.

She woke to the smell of coffee and something sweet. She could hear Ellis in the kitchen. He was humming.

She went to the living room and sat on the couch, head in hands. Ellis came out with her blue apron tied around his waist. Setting a plate on the coffee table, he reached down and put her hand around a mug, looked into her eyes, then backed away.

She sipped. He'd gotten it right. Two spoons sugar and lots of milk. Gaston never made her coffee. She wasn't sure he even knew how. She looked down at her breakfast plate. Ellis made french toast using a bagel. Inside it was an egg with a slice of cheese. There was one little ripe strawberry sitting along side. Ellis reappeared with a vase of dandelions he set quietly on the coffee table and slipped back into the kitchen. Cordelia cried.

She was ravenous, ate through her tears, wiping her running nose on the napkin.

After eating she was unfathomably tired and fell asleep on the couch. When she woke, her plate was gone, she was covered in a blanket, and the house was dark. She'd slept the whole day. Ellis was gone.

Cordelia didn't see nor hear from Ellis that week. He had a big smackdown in Wichita. He'd retired from the ring but trained two big deal wrestlers.

One night Ellis rang the bell. He made lasagna, carried in an insulated pack. They mostly talked about Wichita and what smacked down there. Ellis' guys did as well as predicted, although one of them, Thundering Tappy Vardebeidean, messed up his elbow smashing it into Ape Andrews.

They didn't mention Gaston, but several times during a break in the conversation they held a gaze between them, which they both understood was about Gaston.

After dinner Ellis gave Cordelia a foot massage, packed up his insulated pack, and left.

They didn't talk about Gaston the next night or the night after that. They talked about a lot of things, but not Gaston. They talked about wrestling and the things that held it together and around the edges, like discipline and training and workouts and keeping a good yet aloof relationship with the other wrestlers. They talked about refs and publicity and travel to bouts. They talked about why some guys were one more injury away from retirement. They talked about certain wrestlers, not a small few that had taken too many smacks to the head and ended up having life and reality ebb away in doses every day until things like remembering their dog's name or picking up a coffee cup seemed impossibly exhausting. But they didn't mention Gaston.

They talked about what life could look like after the ring. More and more they talked about walking away from the whole business. This is what Ellis wanted to do. He wanted to chuck the whole thing. He wanted to drop-kick the wrestling life and send it sailing over the turnbuckle.

In between talks, they went to the river, sat on a big rock, dangled their bare feet, and stared gratefully at the clean rushing water as it went about its business en route to the sea.

Sometimes, Ellis wrestled his recliner and Cordelia's recliner into the back of his truck and they went to the drive-in movie. They sat there under the stars watching the film, eating cheese popcorn and drinking Coke.

Often they went to the flea market and spent time trying to find the best piece of junk for under five dollars.

Cordelia never stopped thinking of Gaston. But, more and more she found herself yearning to put her hand in Ellis'. And when Ellis considered a day without Cordelia, a day when she decided to go back to Gaston, he squeezed his eyes shut tight.

But Cordelia wasn't going back to Gaston. Because Gaston was gone and he wasn't coming back. He'd skipped his tenure and gone to the stratosphere where he seemed at home. Joyfully so.

Six months down the road, Cordelia and Ellis went south twenty miles to a big brick facility where Gaston spent his days in an odd but perfect combination of working out, napping, eating, coloring, and watching TV.

In the media room, Gaston was watching a boxing match. He'd stripped off his shirt and rolled up his pant legs. He was prancing around the TV, ducking, swiveling his head from side to side, throwing air punches.

It surprised Cordelia to see how good he looked. She expected to see him lifeless and beaten down. She feared she wouldn't recognize him. This man was fit, robust, energetic. And he was Gaston, gregarious, fun loving, happy and kind. He just didn't quite know what planet he was on.

When Gaston saw Cordelia and Ellis, he sprinted up to them, grabbing Ellis' hand with both of his.

"Hi," he said. "I'm Gaston. I'm a wrestler."

Ellis tightened his stomach against the rush of emotion. Gaston didn't recognize him.

"Hi Gaston, I'm Ellis."

"I'm a wrestler," Gaston said again.

He patted Ellis' shoulder then squeezed his bicep with approval. He patted some more. "Hey, you've got it, man. You could be a wrestler."

Stepping back, looking Ellis over from head to toe, he said, "Are you a wrestler?"

Ellis paused, then said, "Naw, I'm not a wrestler."

Gaston looked at Cordelia and took her hand gently.

"And you beautiful?" He winked at her, shot her a grin. "Are you a wrestler?"

She laughed, "No, I'm just a girl."

Then she looked into the dark sad eyes of Ellis.

"I'm his girl."

Lap of the Moon

Una Nichols Hynum

Tonight the moon is dragging the lake
for memories of you, rays winnowed
by a mild agitation on the water.
Insect and frog choir silent—wind
too, ceases its psalms, oars stashed
in their locks. Sitting on the dock
the way we used to do, I whisper
your name. Willows lean in to listen.
How do I fall out of love with a shadow?
Every path, moonlight or stone
leads to a vanishing point. Sometimes
I wonder if you ever existed.

Love Poem for a Recovering Addict

Una Nichols Hynum

don't let the bastards get you down
each day is a fresh canvas
monet saw with cloudy eyes, van gogh
with his broken heart but look
how they made us see the stars
and water lilies
the cork of your genie bottle
has been removed—each day stretches
into the rest of your life
let's sit here
with the ocean in our laps, our toes
in the silver sand under the long legs
of the pier and watch the sun sink
into the sea—a green flash
a gift like stars and lilies —
what will you show me that I have
looked at all my life
and didn't see

It Popped

Ned Randolph

THIS IS WHAT HAPPENED. I COULD draw a map. Lay out the cars, the gun, bullets, victim, 'hero.' I use the term loosely. It's easy, too much so to lay it out like a bird sees but pop pop pop of the gun and perspective collapses. People duck, lurch their shoulders forward, turn their heads away as if shielding themselves from the shrapnel. Reflexively. Uncontrollably. Incontinently. Someone vomited. The hero would have been embarrassed to know that the picture his mother turned over to the newspaper was from his first high school homecoming dance. Maybe she didn't want to give up one of her favorites. A head shorter than his date, he wore a coat and tie, his cheeks still pumped with baby fat, teeth bracketed in stainless steel, "he will be handsome you can tell," his date's English teacher said when she shared the packet of pictures that an office assistant brought to class. He had been cajoled by friends into the date to hasten his manhood though his sister was appalled at the choice, given her reputation. When he picked her up for the double date, he walked through the front door under the gaze of wall-mounted animals native to Michigan's Upper Peninsula and across the living room's field drab carpet. A scraggly bearded man wearing a green baseball cap sat in a brown lounge chair. He did not introduce himself to the boy or seem to note the awkwardness of him trying to fasten a white corsage on his date and then halting for a stunted pose for a picture taken by her mother. The hero left feeling instinctively defeated. This account was never written down or shared with anyone so his mother had no way of knowing the story of the framed 1986 homecoming photo given to the newspaper to run with his story of his sacrifice. People wanted to know more about him. Some explanation of why he ran toward the chaotic noise against the panicked crowd. Was there any hidden clue in his upbringing? A background in self-defense, knowledge of firearms, a passionate ethos for justice? How would they have reconciled this act with the time he saw a man yelling in the cab of a pickup truck at a woman, grabbing her at the back of her head and pushing her down to the glove box. He ran to the nearest establishment, a restaurant, to report the incident, embarrassed after his adrenaline subsided at his cowardice of passing the problem onto another set of witnesses. Or the time he bolted from the vice principal's office to the cafeteria after hearing a father repeatedly slap his pleading daughter from the adjacent office. The father was the chief of police, and outranked the teachers who came at the request of the boy, whose own father, the town's mayor and police chief's boss, refused to believe the story later that night. But there was something different on this particular Thursday afternoon in March, which no one would ever quite explain. A woman with a gun a good hundred yards from him stood across a male student. He noticed as he was walking with his shoulder bag toward the library a circle of people talking as if they were rehearsing a drama scene for class. Then the popping sound and a victim collapsing in front of her onto her bottom. It was a curious rehearsal. The shooter then turned to a young man on the right who was falling over in an effort to scramble away and fired off more pops. The rest of the circle collapsed outwardly. Faces turned back to the library and ran. Some came toward him in the other direction. Instead of following, he bent low and advanced toward the shooter and her gun, separating himself from danger by parked cars. Nine and a half miles away, a mother—who took prenatal vitamins, eschewed drinking for nine months, and decided at the last minute to forgo natural childbirth (and that's okay) and take the offered spinal tap or whatever they call it now; who worried when her blood tested high for a rare chromosomal disorder, canceled vacations to draw additional blood tests and ultrasounds; and then after the child was born, worried for weeks about the baby's ability to gain weight and feed properly; waking up at all hours of the night to breastfeed the screeching infant whose weight continued to drop, she dedicated the next 18 years of her adult life on early childhood intervention programs to treat dyslexia (discovered among other learning disabilities) through intensive therapy, carefully planned play dates, parent workshops, and at one point going on AFDC food stamps when her husband said he just didn't want to be married to her anymore but still wanted to stay involved in the child's life. His announcement preceded the termination of the child's piano lessons, tennis lessons, private school, and enrollment in regrettable public schools as the mother moved for work, for boyfriends and finally back to Michigan to live with her parents in a decent school district with help from the child's grandmother, who did her best to help keep the child from making mistakes that derail lives and plans, and with enough attention, tutoring, and summer instruction, got her through high school and into Eastern Michigan University, not the most prestigious school but a legitimate college and the type of educational program that offers small classrooms and accessible teachers; allowing the mother, again on her own to assist her now aged mother and attend to the day-to-day worries of a special needs teenager without her ex-husband who for all intents and purposes dropped out of the picture only to show up every other summer or so with a rack full of clothes straight from market and fancy tickets to some gambling resort where he pulls a disappearing act until it's time to return the girl to Dearborn, to provide the kind of supports that she needed throughout her education not from private para-pros or behavioral psychologists but from her flesh and blood—stood up from her desk at a Packard Avenue dental office and keeled over in pain as her daughter's abdomen was pierced by a stray .38 caliber bullet a hundred yards from Halle Library even as she made a wide berth away from an arguing couple that was not wide enough to save her from the collateral damage of bad luck. The shooter, who was 5-ft 9 inches, heavy with a long woolen coat and hat then began walking to the library with the gun drawn rather haphazardly, signifying the possibility of any number of potential moves and outcomes, still the young man advanced on her from behind, now only two car lengths separated. He would have heard the sound of her boots on the newly laid gravel and perhaps her crying or hyperventilated gasping. One girl stood frozen at a table that was signing up volunteers for plasma donations. As the girl with the loosely hanging gun turned toward the plasma volunteer, the coward-come-hero snuck up behind her, grabbed her by the neck and turned her to him, sandwiching the weapon between bodies. As they fell to the ground the gun popped a final time.

Moorings

Fred Longworth

A setter raises a leg to pee
against the lamppost.
An astronomer reaches into pools
of glass and pulls out galaxies.
A serial killer buries a sliver
of his heart beside each corpse.
And James is a whirlwind
in an empty parking lot.
His telephone swears
a vow of silence.
The tag on his mailbox
says "resident."
His living room's a catacomb
for books.
His children have forgotten
where he lives.
His computer is a slaughterhouse
for time.
A stranger stops him on the avenue.
She claims he's nailed boards
across his windows.
She says that once
they were intimate as spam.
He lowers eyes, tries to recall.
The cutting-room bin
is stuffed with snipped-out strips.
He picks one up,
holds it to the light.

Whistling in the Dark

Victoria Melekian

He's a man who plants a tree
and stays to sit in its shade,

but now, his wife gone, the quiet rests
on empty chairs, fills the cups and spoons.

He dumps thirty years in cardboard boxes
and skirts the vacant rooms.

He's moving, but roots have memories.
They're packed and waiting by the door.

Coasting Downhill

Victoria Melekian

On the way home from chemo
we're stopped at the long red light
at Roscoe and Reseda, both of us
looking at the roadside shrine.
It was bigger a year ago.
Now, the cross is gone,
the fresh flowers have been replaced
with plastic ones, and the pinwheel is stuck.
As we drive past, Cheryl says,
"Don't forget me."
I pat her hand and try not to cry.
Five months later her ashes sit
in a vase on her husband's dresser,
it too a small shrine. To its left
is a photo taken just a year ago—
Cheryl's coasting downhill on her daughter's bike,
pink and silver streamers sailing behind.
She's laughing and waving.
Already saying good-bye.

Havoc

Cody Mauro

T HERE ARE SEVENTY WOODEN PANELS ON the ceiling of my bedroom. Maybe more. See, the room has a vaulted ceiling, with two support beams reaching across it, connecting to the walls horizontally at the base of the vault. But the support beams cover up where the boards come together (or don't). Therefore, they may not come together at all and the room may just be lined with long, uncut, singular boards. I can't tell. But I've counted them in every possible way. There's either seventy—that is, thirty-five uncut boards on each side of the ceiling—or there's one-hundred-forty, that assuming the boards come together at each support beam, of which there are two.

I count the panels again, for the fourteenth time tonight, but I try to match the speed of my counting to the pace of my pregnant wife's breathing—she's asleep now, next to me, and has been for a good while now, at least two hours, as that's when her breathing pattern changed. I get all the way to the sixty-sixth board (I always stop on that board and say a quick Hail Mary), when I realize that perhaps I forgot to lock the front door tonight. So I, after a great deal of arguing with myself, stop counting the panels on the ceiling, and throw the blanket off my body, feeling a quick draft from the open window as it ruffles the legs on my tie-dye pajama bottoms. I don't wish to wake Laura, so I tip-toe out of the room and go about my normal security routine: checking to see if the doors and windows are locked, shining a flashlight out of each window (so as to send a warning off to any burglars watching my house), and then I make sure that all the electronics are unplugged because I don't want the house to catch fire. Even though I change the batteries on the smoke alarms twice a week, I don't fully trust them.

I get back into bed, but a thought hits me: what if—by some unholy act of God—I accidentally *unlocked* all the doors? What if I tried to save myself and my pregnant wife but instead I put us in grave danger, practically inviting thieves and burglars and murderers in, and when they saw me flash the light through the windows they thought it was a signal from a friend to come on in so now, as my wife sleeps, as I lie in bed, comfortable and useless, there's a parade of the worst felons Sacramento has to offer climbing through my windows and... and... and....

One. Two. Three. Four. Five.

I count. It calms me when I get anxious. It clears my mind, dissolves my dismay. I turn to Laura. Gently, I shake her, until she stirs apprehensively, like someone who can't believe their alarm clock went off while it was still dark outside.

"Laura, honey. Can you check the locks for me?"

She's facing me now, and the moonlight only illuminates half her face, which upsets me. She's so beautiful I feel cheated by nature that I don't get to see her whole face: the smile countries should fight wars over, narrow eyes, like a cat's, full of mystique and solicitous aggression. "What?" she says, only mustering a whisper.

"The locks. Please, I may have unlocked them. I need you to check. You have fresh eyes, you understand, right?"

"My eyes can barely open right now. What time is it?"

The clock across the room shines bright and fuzzy: 2:36 a.m. "No," she sighs, "just—please—they're fine. Now, go to sleep."

"But I can't sleep if the doors are unlocked," I say. I run my fingers through my hair and grab a patch of hair on the back of my head to let out some tension. I can feel my lips mouthing numbers.

"Russell," Laura says, "no!" She raises her voice and I start counting again. "Christ, honey," Laura says, "I can barely walk as it is—" I'm still counting to myself, my lips making a small pop as my tongue and teeth clack in unison to make my otherwise silent process audible. I think she can hear it because she doesn't finish her sentence.

Laura rolls over, and at first I think she has fallen back asleep because she doesn't move for a moment, but before I can reach over and shake her again, she's out of bed, waddling to the door, her stomach bulging, her feet pounding loud enough to wake up any guests in the house, were we to have some.

When the baby is born, everything will be back to normal. She'll see.

§

I wake up to a sizzling sound. For a second I take a deep breath, just inhaling the smells of bacon, maybe eggs—but then I realize Laura is not next to me in bed. That can't be her in the kitchen. I usually don't let her cook the meals because she makes a mess and then I have to scrub the counters and the floors.

But when I turn the corner, into the smells, into the kitchen, it is Laura. She turns around. I see the smile on her face that I missed out on last night and feel one part relief and one part anger.

"Why are you in the kitchen?" I ask. I try to ignore the little bit of egg on the counter. I try to ignore the crumbs on the edge of the toaster. I try to ignore the smoke from the bacon she probably burnt. But trying so hard to ignore something makes me only notice it more.

"I felt bad," she says, "about last night. For yelling at you." She presents me with a plate of food that she had already set aside. On it, there's some bacon and eggs and a piece of toast. More specifically, there are four strips of bacon that make a sort of Y-shape on the plate laying over the piece of toast with I think butter on it. The eggs are on both sides of the plate. This makes no sense to me. My foods are not only touching, they're not even grouped together. It's anarchy on that plate, and I stare at it for so long and so intently I forget to respond to Laura. "It's a football field," she says, a sincere smile on her face like she just gave a child the present he's been dreaming of. "The bacon is the field goal post, the bread is the touchdown zone. I tried to make a crowd out of the eggs but it didn't really turn out right."

"It's called an end zone," I say. But nonetheless, I thank her. I appreciate the gesture, I suppose.

Laura heads off to take a shower, and I, after spending a good deal of time trying to wade through disappointment—pushing the eggs away from the bacon with two forks and scraping the bread on the side of the plate—I decide breakfast is a lost cause. I've never liked when my food touches, ever, and I wish Laura would have thought about that, because now I'm going to seem like the bad person when I tell her I don't want to eat it. To stave off some of the guilt I don't throw the food away. I try to shuffle it back into the appropriate pans on the stove, putting the bacon back with the bacon and so on (though I did have to throw the bread away). This way, maybe it'll seem like I ate the food, she just made too much.

§

"I'm going to take you to counseling," Laura says in the bedroom later that day.

"No," I say, quietly. "NO!" I scream that. I don't have problems to vent to a stranger for hours a day. My brain just communicates differently than others, and it's unfair for Laura to think that she knows best about me because she doesn't. I know what's best for me, and I know what's best for my son, and I sure as hell won't make him go to counseling or whatever because I'm going to love him just the way he is, and I wish Laura would love me, for the good and the bad, just like we agreed to on our wedding night, and I'm counting but it isn't helping because it can't drown out Laura's shouts of "Please! Please!" and "I'm sorry, so sorry!" as she wraps her arms around me, but it's not helping. One. Two. Three. Four. Five. Six. Seven. Eight.

The air conditioner throbs behind me. I feel the cold air on my neck. Laura has pushed her face into the nook of my neck. "You don't have to go to counseling," she whispers, as if speaking loudly would turn me into a monster, "but I think you should. If not for you, if not for me, then for the baby," she says.

"For my son."

"So will you do it?"

"No. I won't."

Laura leaves the room without looking at me.

§

A few hours later Laura decides she wants to talk to me again. She wants me to go with her to Lamaze class. I don't mind those, to be honest. There's a clear order to them, a rhythm of sorts with the breathing techniques that I like to count along with. It reminds me of my old job at the pretzel factory, pulling the cracked and misshapen pretzels off a conveyor belt for hours, counting each as I take them off the belt. But at Lamaze, instead of the hum of the machinery, it's the hum of idle chit-chat, and instead of counting pretzels, I'm counting breaths.

Today, I'm sitting behind Laura as she breathes in and breathes out: One, two. Three, four. The leader soothes them with words instead of counting. If only these women were more like me, they wouldn't need this class. No, I don't need group therapy, I turn to my life's meter, my metronome, numbers to keep order—I almost feel lucky. Laura shouldn't pity me; Laura should be jealous.

All the women in the room circle around the instructor, a short woman, either overweight or pregnant. I'm unsure. The instructor talks about breathing and pain tolerance and all the men in the room seemed to have tuned out. One guy next to me sits behind his wife and rests his hand on her shoulder and uses the other to hold his cellphone behind her neck. He's following along with live updates of a baseball game. I'm happy he isn't paying attention because I want Laura to notice; I want her to see how good of a father I'll be, how invested I am in her, her happiness, my son's happiness, and not in sports or whatever when it's not appropriate.

She looks back at me over her shoulder and smiles. The same smile I fell in love with when she was a waitress at the diner across the street from my old work. Our son will bring us together. I know it. I don't even have to count to myself to prove it.

§

We leave class. Evidence of the sun leaks over the horizon, stacking colors from yellow to orange to purple, a cotton-candy swirl in the sky. Laura puts her arms around my neck and kisses my cheek.

"Thank you," she says, smiling one more.

"For what?" I ask.

She grabs my hand. "For coming to class with me. Supporting me."

"Of course," I say, grabbing her hand and kissing the back of it. "Anything for you... for our son."

"Anything?" she asks.

I smile, and we get in the car.

§

I'm laying in bed. Tonight I've decided there are one-hundred-forty boards. There's no way they found boards long enough to span the whole roof. I feel so calm, like I'm just an extension of the bed: Lamaze class went so well. Laura and I will work well together as parents.

Laura comes into the room, wearing a pink sports bra and light green shorts. Like a watermelon. Sliding into bed next to me, Laura pulls the covers up to her chin. The bump of her stomach forms a hill in the blanket.

"Russell," she says after a long delay, my name sort of falling out of her mouth as if she was trying hard to lock it up but it forced its way out anyway, "please don't get mad..." I'm bracing myself to get mad as she hesitates, breathes deep, breathes like I breathe when I'm counting, a breath to drown her apprehension. Outside the window, I can hear the wind. Even the earth is breathing. "I made an appointment for you," she says, finally.

"You did what?" I ask.

"Made an appoint—"

I cut her off. "I told you. I won't."

"Please, Russell." She sits up and puts her back to the headboard. "Please. You said you would, the other night, you said you'd do anything."

"Anything but that." A doctor will not help me: when I count, order follows; counting and order are synonymous and no one has yet to prove otherwise.

"Why not?" Laura asks." Tell me why not. A real reason."

I turn to my side away from Laura.

"Answer me, Russell. What will you do when the baby arrives? Huh? What happens when something goes wrong? Am I going to have to do everything while you worry about every single shit it takes giving it some sort of rash? You can't check out and count the hairs on its head every time something doesn't go exactly the way you planned, Russell. You can't."

"There's no reason for it."

It bothers me that Laura doesn't acknowledge we're having a boy. She doesn't respect my gut instincts.

"You can't function Russell. Admit it. You've already lost a job over... *counting.*" She says counting as if it's the most vile word she's heard, a hesitant curse leaving her lips as if she is ashamed to utter it. "I just don't want to lose a husband to it. Or our child to lose a father over it."

"It doesn't bother me—"

"WELL IT BOTHERS ME!" Laura screams. The wind picks up outside the window, blowing the wind chimes that hang outside the window, a tumultuous ringing and banging and clinging and clanging that clouds my thoughts, breaking my concentration on the numbers. I just want to get some peace, to count, to get away from the musical chaos, get away from Laura....

"But why?" I ask, trying to retreat to numbers but finding myself unable to reach ten.

"Because your counting *doesn't* work, Russell. It's useless until *I* get out of bed and check the locks. It's useless until *I* drop the subject and apologize. It's just useless. I don't want to take care of two children, Russell."

If I wasn't angry before, I am now. "I am *not* a child."

"Really?" Laura asks, "if anything doesn't fit into your perfect little world you check out. You're gone. You count, a child throws a tantrum." She pauses, but doesn't look at me, like she's trying to decide if she wants to continue talking or leave it at that. "When will you embrace a change, Russell? How can you live at all if you've planned every second of every day and worry about anything, *anything*, that might change it? I can see it in your eyes now, you're counting, counting because this argument wasn't planned, counting because I'm right about all this, and you've never planned to be wrong."

Laura's crying now and I'm counting—one, two, three, four—but it isn't helping, it isn't helping at all, and it's so silent in the room, so motionless, yet outside the world breathes deep and the wind chimes keep chiming, still going through all of this, and yet I am so still, so ready to get out of bed and run down the hall and shut myself into another room, get peace and quiet and stop being haunted by the breaths of the outside world, the breaths of reality, when all of a sudden, the look of frustration on Laura's face turns to a look of fear, her eyes wide and her nose scrunched like she's in pain, and she starts to mutter, "please, no, not now, not now, NOT NOW," and she throws the covers off of the bed—I'm still counting and it's still not helping—and, holding her belly, she looks down at her shorts, and they're now a darker green by the groin, and water leaks down her leg, a trickle at first, drop, drop, drop, but then a stream, a steady stream that matches the tears coming from Laura's eyes—one, two, three, four—and she pauses and says, "Russell, we need to go."

§

On the way to the hospital, Laura and I do not speak. However, the breathing and sounds of Laura's general agony matches the rhythm of my counting, which serves as an oddly soothing and satisfying orchestra, disrupting the foreboding silence in the vehicle.

We arrive at the hospital and are quickly swept into room iii. I watch as nurses hook Laura up to machinery and medication. I can't handle the chaos inside the room; I can't handle the nurses moving around or the doctor saying *push* and *breathe, push* and *breathe,* so from the chair next to the bed Laura lies in, I turn my attention to the ceiling. I count each of the columns and rows of ceiling tiles and multiply them, and then count each tile individually (for accuracy's sake). There are sixty.

An electrocardiograph machine beeps lightly on the opposite side of the bed. *Beep, beep, beep, beep,* it goes, and I count, one, two, three, four, at first counting the tiles, and then I count the beeps. Now the beeps get faster and faster, so fast I struggle to keep up, and to take my mind off of the numbers

I turn to my wife, my beautiful wife, now red in the face as she screams and pushes, screams and pushes, as the ECG machine goes *beepbeepbeepbeepbeep*.

The doctor wears a mask over his mouth but I still hear him say to a nurse: "It's traverse. Sideways."

"Why was this not corrected?" the nurse asks.

"I'm not sure," says the doctor.

§

Laura screams, louder than ever before now. I wish I could help her, take away her pain, but I realize that right now, I am useless, like a man hiding under his blanket, I am just a man in a chair, a man counting, one, two, three, counting the *beepbeepbeepbeepbeeps* and the tiles on the ceiling to no avail, while the person I need can't help me, doesn't need me, and I think that I should stand by her bedside, maybe, just maybe, hold her hand, look into her eyes, show some compassion, show a benefit to my presence, both in this hospital and in her life, but I can't, I won't, I know how she feels about me now, I can't stop the worry, the images of Laura taking my son and putting him into some black car and then driving away from our house, laughing at me as I try to count my way out of bed in the morning, useless to her, useless to myself, useless to our son, and the laughter hurts my brain along with the *beepbeepbeepbeepbeep* and the shoes shuffling and the screaming and screaming and screaming until I can't take it anymore, with each scream I think more and more of Laura leaving me, or worse, dying in the hospital bed, leaving my son with a father who can't count his way out of the chaos any longer, and I grab my hair, and I close my eyes, and then I take Laura's hand because if I can't be useful to myself I may as well pretend to be useful to her.

Another scream, the loudest of all, and before I know it, the doctor holds a baby, my son, red, bloody, dirty, but alive and mine. He passes it off to a nurse who places him in a white towel and wipes him off, turning the towel a sickening brown color. I imagine someone washing all the blankets covered in blood somewhere in this hospital and cringe.

"We've got a hemorrhage," the doctor says. Nurses begin to bring down oxygen masks, and one calls for a uterine massage. I can't lose Laura. I need Laura. I wish she could count the hemorrhage away. *I* want to count. I want to lean against the wall and just give my problems to the numbers. But the tiles don't interest me. The beeping doesn't interest me. Not right now.

A nurse sits beside me, placing my towel-wrapped baby into my arms. "A beautiful baby girl," she says, "with your eyes."

"A what?" I choke out. I'm so numb, so unprepared for any of this.

I look into my daughter's eyes, green like mine, a nose like Laura's. Then, even though I try pretend to ignore them, I look at the nurses scrambling around the beeping machines and then to Laura on the hospital bed, bleeding. In her position, I would be counting, but numbers and order do not imbue her with strength. To her, right now, or ever, it doesn't matter how many tiles are on the ceiling because tiles or wooden panels don't bring peace, Laura brings the peace in exchange for her own sanity. She may not need me, but I need her. I will do anything for her if she pulls through.

And this time I mean anything.

Winter's Eclipse

Deborah Ramos

Twilight trails stain muddy hooves,
 pounding beneath lunar smoke.

A labyrinth of flesh and fluid
waits for the eclipse to find
the edges, the dim perimeter
of her wanting.

Antlers high, Cimmerian man-elk
ruts to the cool moon center.

Velvet-rich bone, aged virility,
takes her
guards her,
keeps her painfully near.

The Heavy Summer

Rachel Greenberg

WHEN THE SWANS STARTED DYING, ALL at once like a falling of leaves, the hotel managers called in trucks to remove the birds early in the morning before most of the hotel guests were awake. The gray dump trucks lined the shores in the early morning like a row of hulking animals, one for each hotel, their bellies rumbling and their haunches shaking in the cold sea air. The workmen walked through the water in waders or lined the piers with long nets extended downward, scooping away the birds, one at a time, or a few in each net, piling them into the backs of their snorting trucks until the waters were black and clear, dimpled only with the pink of the rising sun.

By midday, the beaches would be filled with content tourists, no wiser to what the workmen did in the mornings, but the effort to hide the reports of the swans was enormous. The local fishermen from the villages, who were on their boats each morning before the trucks arrived, knew about the massive kills of birds and word spread quickly among the islanders that the dead birds had bloated necks as though they had swallowed poison, and that where the corpses clumped together beneath the piers and along the shore, the surface of the water would turn gray and foamy like dishwater.

The villages of the island, where the native peoples lived in low-roofed, brightly-colored houses, were spread around the edges of the downtown tourist district and acted as a barrier for the city and suburbs against the more treacherous points of the coastline and the openings of the old-growth forests where long heavy branches and vines hung down over the village rooftops. Some of the villages had one or two paved roads leading to the center of a square or marketplace, but even those roads remaining were pockmarked and crumbling and difficult to maneuver, most often, ending with an unremarkable church or gas station dropped between the leaning palm trees.

During the season that would later be known as the Heavy Summer, the villagers bore first witness to every change of the island. With no hotel managers to secretly clean their beaches every morning, the villagers quickly learned to add the daily task of clearing away the dead birds to their before-dawn chores to prepare for the tourists who would walk down their bumpy streets at midday to buy the shell jewelry and colorful scarves they hung along their porches.

It also seemed to the villagers that, over time, the waters were changing color to the swampy gray that the fishermen first saw only around the dead birds. Many of the young people in the village were confident that they were dealing with a force of divine will, and for that reason were unafraid. They grasped after old customs, pointed to the ancient stone and wooden sculptures that dotted their shores like sentinels against the elements, their mouths carved open with grimaces of ivory teeth, searching for an identity that would mean protection from the wrath of old gods. In any bar and around any card game, there was always one young man who would proclaim, growing louder as the evening went on, that this, surely, was a statement of warning against the invaders of their lands, that something ancient and fearsome was striking back against the abusers. The loud young man, caught up in his own talk, would not notice as the older men lowered their eyes or shook their heads and exchanged cautious looks, while the women sitting on the porches worked silently on their weaving, listening to what the men said inside, letting their unspoken fear grow heavy between them.

The old in town did not speak of the changes, and the young said that they had grown jaded to the crowding on the shoreline by a steady inward trickle, generations long, of colonization. But the old sat silently on their fear that when the space between heaven and earth shrinks and the skies meet the seas and the earth quakes as though beset with fever, that there are none safe or spared. And those between the young and the old knew that faith is a mighty tool in an unwinnable war.

By the time the board of tourism took notice, it was too late for them to sit in air-conditioned rooms discussing preventative measures. The loss of the swans, a favorite subject for tourists' photos and a draw for bird lovers all over the world, could represent a serious loss of tourist dollars, and could eventually lead to legal ramifications if no environmental protective measures were taken.

Local newspapers and magazines ran articles about the birds and their mysterious deaths with investigative reports on the impact of the sugar refinery, the island's most productive factory, on the water and air quality. Others raised concerns about the burden of sewage runoff on the local ecosystem, and pointed fingers at the downtown hotels and the cruise liners that parked along the shore.

Next was the sand, which all at once grew cold, as if the sun had never risen on the day. It took the tourists by surprise when, removing their sandals, they found it chilled as a fresh-fallen snow and heavy as though with the condensation of the night air. The tourists stood about looking at each other and shrugging until each followed the lead of another and carried on with their beach day; for after all, the sun was still shining and the waves were still lapping up onto the shore and they had paid for a vacation.

At the university, talk shifted from questions of runoff and contamination to questions of tectonic activity and changes in weather systems. Claims were made that sudden and natural shifts in weather systems and tectonic plates could produce temperature change and maybe even a train of ecological cause and effect that could produce the bird deaths. Opponents suggested that the overwhelming pressures of a warming Earth could not be overlooked. A conference was convened at the university with visiting scholars on seismic activity, global environmental change, tropical ecologists, marine biologists, geologists, astronomers, and ornithologists. A professor from a university in Boston spoke of the impact of environmental disaster on economies that depend heavily on tourism. Petitions were written and sent to congressman and grant makers and generous foundations and Fortune 500 businesses.

Among the islanders, children began to develop a certain fear of the ground, as though that which was killing the seas and freezing the land were rising up from below like some ancient sleeping creature in the core of the Earth, pushing up against the ceiling of its confinement, which had held it down since before creatures crawled on its back.

Slick gray seals began to crowd the boulders on the beaches, shivering in the sun, unnerved by the cold sand and disgusted by the foul tasting water and bloated bland fish. Mothers abandoned their pups to swim for warmer waters, and tourists batted at the wide-eyed dying animals that could not understand which way to turn.

When the fishermen, who had known many seasons of bad catches and low counts, began to pull up empty nets and pots, the islanders released the panic that had been welling up within them, and the communal grief was like a dam collapsing and the fear of a fatal winter set it. The hotels and restaurants shifted their orders from the villagers to off-island sources, and the crates coming in off the cargo planes multiplied and the deliveries became more frequent.

It soon came to be known that the sugar refinery, the prize of the island economy, had been quietly purchased several years prior by a certain brand known worldwide for over-farming and cap trading. Many of the well-meaning colonists began to boycott the sugar, while the university began an intensive study into island farming practice and pesticide use.

Except for the fishermen, who tried day after day to reel in a catch, the islanders no longer went into the waters. Children began to tell stories of ghostly gray creatures with dripping oily skin and features as indistinct as lumpy mounds of sand that walked the shore at night like widows looking out to sea. And the adults dreamt at night of a poisonous oily film on the ocean and the pockets of thick gray foam that collected along the piers and they imagined their own throats bloating from the inside out from one gulp of toxic ooze.

On Saturdays and Sundays, tourists continued to line the broken roads that led to the villages with rented cars and bicycles to visit the markets to buy baskets woven from palm fronds, tapestries and rugs streaked with bright inks, and jewelry made from shells smoothed soft. There might be a few tables where villagers sold flowers and fruits of the island, but mostly, the market was filled with tables of plastic toys and tee shirts, ordered in bulk, meant to turn a profit. But with the fishermen pulling in lighter and lighter nets, the villagers started to rely more heavily on the small amounts they collected from the tourists on the weekends.

Tourist season did not slow, and the families of four after families of five never seemed to worry about the sand or the seas, even later when the missing birds and absent fish left the strands of seaweed to grow into long thick tendrils that clogged the shore with mats of weeds, crawling with flies and reeking of rot.

A season of strong summer storms began, and all along the waterfront the lighting reached down to the ocean as though to quiet it. There began a steady rain that went on for days until the piers sank with heavy boards, and the shoreline crept up on the streets, and the long fingers of the waves reached the low porches of the villagers' homes seated close to the waterline, as though to remind them they had been too long out of the water.

The islanders, some with old religion and some with new and most with a combination, prayed in the white clapboard churches that shook in the wind, and some cursed the men who did this to them and some cursed the men who let it happen, and no one dared to imagine what kind of agency there could be beneath the sea that reached upward and the sky that reached downward, and punished the faithful and the sinner alike.

When the storms broke after a week of heavy rain and dark skies, the islanders were struck to see the sun rising one morning into a soft pink sky, as though it had never left. And the trucks were back, too, huddled up shoulder to shoulder against the shore, accepting spoonful after spoonful of thick water, dead bird and fish, a bitter medicine swallowed dutifully and without question. Cautiously, the villagers returned to their resilient land, while the tourists who had spent the rainy week on board games and movies and extended meals, returned to the beaches, kicking away clots of tangled seaweed as they went.

The Day Cell Phones Killed 6.2 Billion People

Marisol Benter

All over the globe noses were touching tiny blue screens,
grease wiped from fingers to heavily starched clothes. Clicking.

Pods of suits moved as one tumultuous black sea, blue lights
in their ears, sense gone from their eyes. *Terminate; Sales; Close.*

Tiny knives peeled back thin pieces of cornea, lasers shaping
soft tissue into computer perfection. So the letters were clear.

Meals were silent, heads bowed over humming black boxes,
food gray and cold on white plates. Paperless messages.

A girl sat at the ocean, her feet hanging off the dock above water.
She held a glowing object in her hands. Her eyes blurred.

There was a moment, then a rapid blinking, and every alloy
in the world began to heat up into flame. Simultaneous expulsion.

I was in the forest when I felt the ground move.
Birds stilled in the sky.

Watching the Ponies Roam

Marisol Benter

Seven hummingbird feeders twirl
from young sturdy-slim branches
of this California Sycamore, and I
can't decide if my feet belong here
in the leaves or down on the trail.
Pepper colored cows stare across
Big Sur fog knowing the blue line
of the Pacific is just a stretch ahead,
walnut groves over their backsides,
their urgency undetectable, and I want
that. I want to know what they know.
No more. No less. Just what grass
has to offer. I want to stay here
till the jay gets testy and throws pebbles
at me, till I see each hummingbird's
chest rise and fall, still turquoise wings,
and feet plant for just one second,
till our friends have fallen asleep on the ground,
noses to the sky, till the peach sun dips
for the last time on this trip to the Redwoods,
and we don't have to think about leaving.

After Dark

Mary Beth Dodson

I come to the swing after dark
To hear the night.
To listen to the locust
Sing a slow cadence.
Everything is winding down
In October. The grasses draw
Damp lines on my bare feet
On my flight forward, upward
Into the near-silent blackness.
The dark is friendly, blending
The lilies, the ageratum, the Blue
Spruce into one mounting shadow,
Erasing any weeds, any unevenness.
Stars salt the sky above the ash,
But where is the moon?
I round the house, the path
Between the brick that still holds
The afternoon warmth, and the grape
Vine that overlaps the fence,
In search of the moon.
I find it in the southwest,
Tipped back, only half there.
It rocks on the slope of the house
Down the alley.
I could reach it in an easy climb.
But I'll only admire it from here.
Some things are too perfect to touch.

You See 'Ums

Judy Geraci

Y OU SEE HIM WALKING DOWN THE street. The black man with long, loping legs, a costume cat tail in one hand and his balding pate in the other. Shaking his head, mumbling, he suddenly looks up and stares right through you as if he heard you noticing.

"I got problems," he says, stroking his marbled fuzz. "I got problems," he repeats, waiting for an answer. You nod, say you're sorry, and move on. Later in the day, you see him again as you pull up the rise of the winding canyon road in your quiet suburban neighborhood. He's straddling the double yellow line, frozen in the street with his shirt stripped, and his tail lost. He appears as a two-legged moose with terrifyingly open eyes as his hands are outstretched on either side of his temples. You cringe, thinking about all the cars zooming up the Juniper dip. You imagine screeching tires, slamming brakes. Even if you never go to church, or you're not sure what you believe, or you know full well that you don't believe, you find yourself praying that he won't get hit.

You see her waiting for the bus. The lady with the wide-brimmed hat, every inch of her apparel pressed and her pants sharply creased. Even the red handkerchief tied around the handle of her straw purse is square-knotted in a perfect party bow. Talking to the air, her hands fly and her head shakes in invisible argument. When you get closer, you see that she has a patch over one eye, but not exactly—not a black patch or orthopedic beige. Not a patch held over her eye by an elastic band, but a patch taped to the front of her glasses. A homemade patch with an elaborately inked eye drawn with thick, curling lashes. And under the eye, neatly printed block letters: "JUST AIN'T WORKING."

You see him standing on the corner, yelling. Just yelling. At a girl he loves or used to love or wants to love, but she's walking away. She walked away five minutes ago and her back is a parenthesis in the distance. Away, away she goes, but he can't stop yelling. After she's gone, he still sees her. He wants her to come back. He's crying with the bends, pushing his hands around his ears, raking his hair and pulling it hard to make the pain in his scalp outshout the pain inside. She's gone, but she still hears him, and when he pulls his hair out, she collapses on the shoulder of a stranger.

You feel her on your shoulder. She has walked into your workplace: red eyes, dark circles, and a collapsed soul on her face. She says, "I've never ever done this, but I need a place to cry on and your shoulder looks so strong."

You look into a mirror, and your forehead is a blue square, and your nose is softly blurring. Your cheeks are purple circles that are whirring, purring, stirring. You are channeling Picasso, and the Cubists have you covered. You peer deep at your reflection and you see yourself discovered. Now you can only speak in rhyme.

Still, you see them at the bus stop, at the laundry, in the pet shop. You see them at the station, in the park, at the backstop. You are scared, you are revolted, and you find yourself unbolted. Thinking Jesus and compassion. Thinking kindness, loving action. Thinking, praying, and you know, there but for the grace you go.

Home Fires

Laurie Richards

O NE CIGARETTE LEFT—THE LAST UNTIL HER military allotment arrives. A paperback lies unopened on her lap. "It's about hope and poverty," her mom said, but Ruth hasn't reached the hope part.

"Right now I'll hope for my check," she tells the quiet house. "And a letter from Chuck." She thrums her fingers against the sofa's arm. At first, the checks came on time, but with trains fighting Iowa snowstorms, arrival dates slipped. Chuck hasn't written since his ship got posted to Guam only days after the U.S. ousted the Japanese in August. How do other women bear long, silent months and stretching those allotment dollars like they're gum?

She peers outside. Dark clouds slash the eastern sky, but no sign of the postman.

The truck from Sioux City Coal pulls into the alley. She doesn't have enough money for both coal and food, so she'll try bluffing. 'I'll bring cash tomorrow, promise.' Her bluffs worked pretty well with the grocer until her last visit when he said, "No more credit."

She grabs her purse and pulls on her coat, a dark plaid that hides spill spots, stains from coffee and Emma's messy fingers. She folds the cuffs under to cover a moth hole. Outside, the wind whips through the wool and sends a shudder into her blood. The truck parks, and a worker in a soot-covered storm coat jumps out and walks toward the coal chute. The driver, a bulky man with a smudged face and a dark scar through his upper lip, gets out and turns to Ruth. The guy doesn't look like he'd be sympathetic if his own mother needed coal.

Shivering, Ruth stands with her hands and her purse behind her back.

"Payment on delivery, Mrs. Mason," the driver says.

She looks down the street with a hope that she'll see the postman, bag slung over his shoulders. A taxi rounds the corner and pulls up in front of her bungalow. Jimmy Morton rolls down his window and waves. She turns to the coal man so Jimmy won't hear what she's saying.

"My allotment check's due. I'll bring in the money soon as I get it."

The driver rubs his chin with a hand gloved in dirty canvas and leaves another smudge. "No cash, no coal."

A car door slams. Jimmy's probably heard him. Probably going to butt in.

"Please," she says to the driver, "a blizzard's coming." As if he can't see for himself.

He motions to his helper. "Get in the truck, Al." Al stops whatever he's been doing to ready the load.

Ruth weighs her worries. Will the kids get sick faster from hunger or from cold?

Beside her, Jimmy's digging into a pants pocket and tells the guy to go ahead. He puts his other hand on her shoulder, and she brushes it off. She glances around. Are the neighbors watching? The coal man is. He gives her that up and down look she sometimes gets from men.

The wind slams a sting against her cheeks. "No," she says, "I'll pay now."

Al again busies himself with the load, and she turns to Jimmy. He's holding his cap under his arm and with the other hand, he's running a black comb through his hair while the wind fights him. Even in high school, Jimmy had much pride in his thick waves. He would've hated the butch Chuck got from the Navy.

"I didn't call for a cab," she tells him.

He shrugs. "You always gotta go to the store. I'll give you and the kids a ride."

"They're down for their naps."

The radio in his cab crackles, and he dashes toward it. After a few words into the speaker, he waves. "I'll come back."

She can't put a finger on what it is about Jimmy—why she has to ration what she'll accept from him. If she takes him up on his offers, will she be going through a door best kept closed? Ever since Chuck got called up, her life has come down to slim choices. Heat—or food. Rent—or food. Warm clothes for the kids—or food. Kindness from an old friend like Jimmy—or what? Is it kindness?

At least Chuck isn't hungry or cold. At least the Navy feeds him regularly and stations him some place warm. "There's a beach in Guam, and we'll get to swim in the ocean," Chuck had written in his last letter. She's never seen a beach, but it's winter in Guam too, and she shivers at the thought of a splash into freezing water.

The coalmen dump a quarter ton through the chute. She steps back to avoid the dust that reaches her anyway, and she coughs. The driver hands her a ticket and gives her change after she doles out the last of her dollars. She stands in the alley fingering the dime and three pennies remaining. Enough for milk, but nothing else. She sees the postman on her block, bundled in his regulation overcoat, hat and muffler. At other houses, he lifts the mailbox lids and slips envelopes inside. When he gets to her place, she's waiting with her hand out.

"No checks today, Mrs. Mason."

Her cheeks feel chilled. She didn't realize her tears had been so close to spilling out, so ready to brave freezing into tiny icicles on her skin. "No other mail?" she says.

He glances at the sky, and she does too. Gray-streaked clouds move overhead. "You better get inside," he says.

For the rest of the day, playing with Emma and Dorothy takes her mind off the empty mailbox—empty of money, empty of words from Chuck. He seemed no different from anyone else when they met during the Depression. Everyone had trouble laughing then, but other men got back to their easy ways. Now she doubts Chuck ever had easy ways. Emma is too young to miss affection from her daddy, but Dorothy clamors for it. Before he left to be a sailor, she ran to the door whenever Chuck came home, and she climbed on his lap the minute he sat down. If he let her, that is. Now Dorothy draws pictures of him with the brightest crayons and asks every day when will her daddy be home.

Ruth sleeps in the middle of the bed these nights. She's tired of the loneliness in the room, but wasn't it there before? When she stretches her arms out, she recalls how Chuck's body sunk into the mattress, how he offered his cheek for her kiss goodnight before he rolled toward the wall. In the mornings, he was up and out—no hug, no kiss.

Overnight the blizzard delivers two-foot drifts that cover her sidewalk.

For breakfast, she gives Emma her bottle and feeds Dorothy oats with only water, leaving enough cereal for one more meal. She sets Emma in the playpen. Dorothy picks up "The Ugly Duckling" coloring book and pulls a red crayon from the tin.

"Can I use this on the sky, Mama?" she says.

Ruth she pretends a smile and summons her 'fun' voice. "Of course, my pretty swan."

Her swan giggles and scrawls away.

"I have to do some laundry, honey. Make sure Emma stays in the playpen." Ruth doesn't like turning her four-year-old into a babysitter, but the basement's too dirty and cramped for the kids. Dorothy nods as she streaks red in the sky over the duck pond.

Ruth opens the basement door, and the musty smell and coal dust rush at her. She fills the furnace, stokes it, and then wipes black dust off the Maytag and dumps in a load of diapers. She'll clean the clotheslines when the load is ready to hang. By then the dust will have finished settling. Chuck strung lines across the basement before he left for basic training. She'd told him then they were too high.

"I said shoulder height. I meant my shoulders, not yours."

He patted her hips. "A little stretching won't hurt."

Everything in her life is a stretch. Money. Cigarettes. Food. Smiles for her babies.

In his last letter, months ago, he said he won at poker, and he'd stop home and give her some of his winnings before shipping out to Guam. For a few days, Ruth's loneliness had left her when she thought of spending time with him. She and the kids had walked a mile to the train station, Dorothy at her side and Emma in the carriage.

"Daddy's home," Dorothy kept saying as she rocked the carriage, making Emma squeal.

Rain was falling in sheets when the train pulled in, and Ruth huddled on the platform with the kids. Dorothy spotted her daddy in every soldier who stepped off, but not one of them was Chuck.

"They should've let him come," Dorothy said as they marched back home.

"How am I supposed to keep the home fires burning?" Ruth later asked her mom. "When he writes, it's only a few lines and when he can come to see us, he doesn't."

Her mom said, "Wherever he is, he'll be faithful to you, Ruth. You don't have to worry about that."

"There's more than one way to be unfaithful, Mom," Ruth had said.

That was two months ago, and she hasn't heard what happened—nothing at all. Why didn't he make it home? If he'd been hurt, wouldn't the Navy let her know?

Ruth puts the kids down for their naps, and then shovels enough snow to clear a path to other paths that will lead to the store. After that, she stretches out on the sofa and twirls her last cigarette between two fingers. She sniffs it and reaches into her pocket for matches. No. She has to resist. She sniffs the cigarette again, breathes deeply and pretends she's inhaling. If the check doesn't come soon she'll need this last cigarette even more. How will she reward herself later for this sacrifice now? A chicken? She takes a deep breath as if she can smell the chicken frying.

A picture of Chuck sits on the end table. His dark eyes, set deep above high cheekbones, look out with a gentleness that matches the slight upturn of his lips. Her husband shares a comfortable homeliness with Abraham Lincoln. When she met Chuck, she thought his emotions would match the gentleness of his eyes. Now she knows she misread him. He wasn't gentle; he was numb. She'd like to reach down to where he knots his feelings into a tight ball. She'd pull that ball out until it floated like a balloon, and they'd laugh together about how light it is. But Chuck never finds much to laugh about. And the knot stays inside him.

Dozing, she dreams the wind is rising, rattling the porch screens, jiggling the mailbox. She dreams the kids are playing in snow with no clothes on. She jerks awake. It's not yet three, but clouds shut out the sun. She's slept past time for the mail.

The box hangs from two nails near the porch door. Its black paint has peeled away, exposing a rough surface. The lid has rusted into a tilt. With a push at the front door, she reaches for the box without stepping outside. She lifts out a letter from Chuck's Cousin Betty, probably to firm up the plans for her visit next week. Betty is welcome company and a help with the kids.

No check.

In the kitchen, steam from her coffee cup mingles with wetness forming in her eyes. Why can't she be satisfied? She savors a sip of the coffee-flavored chicory and picks up Betty's letter. Thank god, only three more days before the visit. Ruth slips a table knife under the envelope's flap, but the sound of someone creeping near the top of the stairwell reaches her. Dorothy is the only one who would creep. As usual, circumstances have decided matters, and Ruth will have to put off reading the letter. Life can turn a corner unexpectedly because she sips her coffee too long.

She props the envelope in front of Chuck's picture and at the stairwell, pokes her head around the corner. In a whisper, she calls out, "Is that my swan?"

Dorothy's sweet, small voice makes Ruth smile. "Can I get up, Mommy?"

Ruth leans into the dark, able to make out Dorothy huddled at the top step. She tries taking the stairs silently. Emma, baby, don't wake up yet. She first needs to get Dorothy bundled into warm clothes for a trip to the store.

She whispers, "Let's get dressed, honey."

Emma's already awake, but happily playing with her fingers. Ruth removes her from the crib and changes her on Dorothy's bed.

By the time both kids are ready, hail is tapping against the window.

"Hear that, Mommy." With a wide grin, Dorothy points to the window. She always likes listening to a good storm, but she won't want to step one foot outside. They won't make it to the store.

A loud horn honks twice, and Dorothy runs to the window. A staccato honking starts, timed to the beat of 'shave and a haircut,' then a pause and more honks for the 'two bits.' Only one guy would make music with his horn, loudly announcing his visit to the whole neighborhood.

The hail is pelting hard. She should've asked someone to watch the kids while they were napping. She could've gotten milk then. Kool-Aid might do for Dorothy, but not Emma. The front door creaks and Jimmy's nasal "Hullo?" reaches through the house. Ruth carries Emma and follows Dorothy in a clopping procession down the stairs. Jimmy pokes his head around the doorway at the bottom.

"Hi, kidlings." He reaches out and tousles Dorothy's hair. She giggles as she edges around him, even though his body fills most of it the doorway. Jimmy backs off with a smiling wink at Ruth. She likes a smile that appears so easily. He's five years younger than Chuck, but the draft board rejected him for a reason he explained by pointing to his feet. "Flat and 4F," he said. His face is colorless from an Iowa winter, not like the tan Chuck must be getting on a beach in Guam.

When she reaches the last step, Jimmy takes her chin in his hand and peers at her. "You doing okay?" His voice is so kind, so sincere, she feels guilty as she slaps his hand away.

"I'm fine." She made sure her tone was neutral, but she's not feeling neutral; she's feeling overwhelmed like when she had to bluff the grocer, and it didn't work. She needs her husband, not this guy.

She puts Emma in the playpen, and Jimmy sets his cabbie's hat on the nearby end table, then sinks into Chuck's brown armchair and lights a cigarette. He offers his pack of Camels to her. She catches herself staring at it. Finally shakes her head.

"What are you doing here?" She walks to the window and taps her knuckles against the glass. "Isn't this a busy time for cabbies?"

"No," he says. "People just stay cooped up inside. So I stopped by for something warm." He pats his knee as if she should sit there, and she scowls.

Dorothy won't get his meaning, but Ruth tells her, "Play something. Get the Crayolas and coloring books." Dorothy moves to the end table where the crayons sit under a copy of Longfellow's poems.

Jimmy exhales circles of smoke. "Need anything from the store?"

"You should be in your cab. Dispatch might be trying to reach you."

He nods toward her near-empty pack of Kools on the end table. "I'll bring some later."

Ruth points to Chuck's picture. The lie is easy. "He's coming home on furlough."

"Sure," he says, "but not tonight."

She peers at him. "Not tonight for you either."

He takes his hat, grips an arm of the chair and rises. "I'll bring some cigarettes."

"Don't," she says and folds her arms in front of her. She doesn't walk him to the door. Before he opens it, he runs his fingers through his hair and then puts his cap on. He pulls his collar up and bolts down the steps, yelling "Goodbye, kids."

Why can't he be less boisterous? The neighbors probably clocked his visit to the precise second.

Dorothy is coloring, and Emma is fussing. Ruth sighs, knowing things will be better during Betty's visit. She picks up Emma and sits on the sofa.

"I'll read to you while you draw," she says and Dorothy grins.

"Hiawatha." Dorothy waves an arm, saying "Hiawatha" over and over.

Ruth picks up the aged copy of Longfellow's poems. She reads aloud about the Indian who was alone in heaven until the lucky warrior came upon a maiden when "the fog lay on the river, like a ghost that goes at sunrise."

Dorothy looks up from her coloring. "Is that the woman with yellow hair like mine, Mommy?"

It isn't, but Ruth sees no need to disappoint. "Yes, honey. He loved a maid with hair just like yours."

Dorothy stops coloring, her blonde eyebrows crinkling. "Why is she a ghost, Mommy?"

Ruth closes her eyes. Disaster lurks even in the most well-intended fib. "She wasn't a ghost, honey. The poet says the fog on the river looks like a ghost." Dorothy shrugs and bends over her coloring again, so Ruth stops talking about the ghost at sunrise. She sets the book down. Emma's quiet, and Ruth puts her back in the playpen and tells Dorothy to be good while she fixes dinner. In the kitchen, there's an unopened box of vanilla wafers on the table.

Jimmy.

Why is he so bold he walks through her house and leaves a cheap bribe in her kitchen? She'll give them back. Maybe right in his pasty face.

"Hey, cookies." Dorothy holds out her hand. A slim choice again. Stand on her pride or give Dorothy a treat? Life has too many corners, too many slim choices. It's only cookies. Something he did for the kids.

"Not before supper, sweetie."

They eat canned string beans and tomato soup. Emma gets mashed carrots and the last of the milk.

Everyone gets vanilla wafers.

And the hail turns to snow. And the snow will keep falling, and the world will look soft and white in the morning, but beneath it all, ice will lurk.

Dorothy lets Ruth wipe crumbs from her chin, and says, with a knowing nod of her head, "We're gonna have cake when Cousin Betty comes."

Ruth remembers the letter.

She lifts Emma from the high chair, hustles everyone into the living room, and picks up the envelope. "Let's see what your daddy's cousin has to say." She raises her eyebrows to inspire their excitement at the very thought, and they respond with satisfying giggles. When she unfolds the paper, the words "sick" and "can't come" fly at her, and she drops the letter on her lap. Disappointment presses on her like wet wool.

Dorothy tugs on her sleeve. "What does she say, Momma?"

Ruth stands up. "She's says it's your bedtime."

After she tucks the children in and does the dishes, she sinks into the armchair and takes Betty's letter out to finish it.

We got a note from Chuck today. He said he's been swimming in the ocean and getting tan. He asked me to let you know he's okay and thinking of you and the kids.

Ruth screams "no" at the walls, not caring if the kids wake up. Maybe they should learn that their dad doesn't care a hoot about them. She screams again. She balls up the letter and throws it across the room. She balls up the envelope. Tosses it hard. She digs her nails into her palms as she looks around for something else. There's the tattered book of Longfellow poems, but she pauses. It's her mother's copy. When she was young and her mother read "Hiawatha" to her, Ruth had seen herself as the maid who captured the heart of the great warrior. It wasn't until Ruth first read it to Dorothy that she realized her own mom had skipped the part where the warrior was "false and faithless" with the beauteous maid.

She turns off the lights and stretches out on the sofa with only loneliness to cover her.

The porch steps creak, and soft taps of "shave and a hair cut" reach her. She rises and creeps toward the window, draws back the drape. A ribbon of light travels to where he stands in shadow, and the tendril of a soft glow falls on his pale features. A carton of Kools pokes out from the grocery bag he cradles in one arm. He shifts, and the light reveals the top of a milk bottle.

"The ghost that goes at sunrise," she whispers and opens the door.

How I Survived an Assassination Attempt on My 13th Birthday

Scott Barbour

O N MY 13TH BIRTHDAY MY DAD brings out a cake with a baseball diamond and little plastic baseball players on it even though a) I'm not seven, and b) I don't even play baseball since I was banned for life from Little League after my so-called bat rampage.

Everyone starts singing "Happy Birthday," and I jump to my feet and stand against the wall because I know the so-called cake is wired with C4 or laced with E coli or anthrax or the bubonic plague. Or maybe the candles are mini sticks of dynamite that'll blast my face off when I make my wish and lean in.

My mom says, "What a cute cake!" and reaches for a finger full of frosting and I shout, "Nooooooo!" and slap her arm before the frosting touches her lips. Then I throw the cake on the kitchen floor and stomp on it with both feet to make sure it's dead.

My dad grabs me from behind and I'm kicking his legs and squirming, and even though my fighting skills are superior, he controls me with his alien powers.

He's saying, "Jimmy, count to ten," and my mom's saying, "Can't we have a normal birthday just this once?" and my grandma's grabbing my dad's arm and saying, "Let go of him!" and her boyfriend William is grabbing her arm and saying, "It's best to stay neutral in delicate family matters," and my dad says, "Count to ten! Count to ten!" and I know the only way he'll let go is if I get still and count to ten slowly, it's not like this doesn't happen every day.

I stop and count to ten and he lets me go and I say, "Great, now I have to decontaminate!" and head for the back door and my dad says, "Now you have to mop the floor, you mean!"

I go outside and turn on the hose and kick off my shoes and Rudy our dog starts licking the chocolate cake off them and I say, "No, Rudy!" but it's too late, I'll have to watch him for symptoms.

It's a cold October night and the water's freezing but it's important to decontaminate quickly following any alien-human contact, so I strip naked on the grass and hose myself down starting at my head and working my way to my toes.

When I'm done I'm shivering and goose bumpy. My dad's standing by the door with a big orange towel and I consider hopping the fence and making a run for it, but it's not safe to leave the perimeter without my nunchucks.

I shout, "Leave the towel on the steps and back away slowly!" but my dad comes toward me holding out the towel like he's going to suffocate me.

I throw my shoes at him, but he ducks one and blocks the other and then grabs me in the towel and carries me inside like I'm a kid.

Back in the kitchen he lets me go and says, "Get dressed and mop the floor," and I say, "I'll be needing a hazmat suit and a Geiger counter," and he says, "I'll give you a mop and a bucket."

Luckily, there was no skin-on-skin contact when my dad picked me up, so I don't have to re-decontaminate. I go to my room and change into my desert camo pants and Metal Mulisha tee shirt and come back to the kitchen. My grandma has a box of cake mix out and is dumping it into a big metal bowl. "You can't have a birthday without cake," she says.

In case you don't know my grandma, she's super old like any grandma but she wears jeans and leather boots and a Harley Davidson tee shirt and has a braid of gray hair going down her back. The funny thing is, her boyfriend William dresses the same way and even has the same gray braid down his back. The difference is he also has a gray beard and he's fatter. Also, when they ride his Harley he wears a leather jacket that says "Aficionados of Existential Despair" on the back, and my grandma wears one that's blank because she says she's no one's "old lady."

When William gets up for a can of Bud, which he does about every ten minutes, he walks stiff and the keys attached to his belt jingle and his leather boots squeak.

My dad slides a bucket across the floor and hands me the mop and says, "Get to work," and I say, "why do I have to clean up the remains of your failed execution device," and my grandma says, "You're gonna make him mop the floor on his own birthday?" and my mom says, "He should be having a party."

William says, "I believe that the events of the past half hour could reasonably be characterized as a party," and my grandma says, "Ha! Some party!"

My mom says, "Music... fun..." She's sitting at her usual place at the kitchen table wearing her baggy brown around-the-house sweater and smoking a cigarette and drinking coffee like always. She's staring at the smoke rising from her cigarette toward the ceiling with that dreamy look on her face like she's imagining her family the way it's supposed to be. "Dancing..." she says. "Pizza... Ice cream... Girls..."

Everyone gets quiet and the word "girls" sort of hangs in the air, and for a second I have this vision of a party with all my friends and Cynthia and her friends in the basement with the stereo playing some of that Usher R&B crap for the ladies. There are about 25 problems with this picture, starting with the fact that my friends all betrayed me one by one, and Cynthia is intimidated by my awesome masculinity and pretends not to like me.

William says, "Yes, an interest in the fairer sex would be quite appropriate for a male of young master James's age."

My dad starts to walk out of the room, which he does a lot when William starts talking, but then he stops and says, "You know what, William? First, his name's not young master James. It's Jimmy. And second..." My dad stands there staring at William with two fingers sticking up in the air looking like he can't think of what to say. "Aren't you due for another beer?" he finally says.

William says, "Why, yes, my fine country gentleman, another beer of the Budweiser variety would be quite superlative."

My dad's face gets that red splotchy look it gets when he's about to blow. He leaves the room but then he comes right back because a) I'm his personal slave and he can never leave me alone for five seconds, and b) he knows a wet mop is a dangerous weapon in my hands and he fears I'll use it to take his place as the alpha male of the house.

The first thing he does when he comes back is criticize my mopping skills. "You're just sloshing it around, you're just making a big mud puddle. Remember what I taught you, you have to wring it out once in a while."

My grandma says, "If you're so great at it, why don't you do it yourself?" and cracks an egg in her bowl of cake batter.

I add more soapy water to my puddle, expanding it under the dishwasher, making a chocolaty pond.

My grandma says, "He shouldn't be mopping the floor on his birthday, anyway." She stands in the middle of the room with her hands on her hips. My dad stares back at her with his arms across his chest. He's still wearing his work clothes—tan slacks and a blue polo shirt with a Couch Warehouse patch. He's bigger than everyone in the room, even William, but I still think my grandma could take him. I lean on my mop to watch the fight.

My dad says, "He's 13 now. He needs to start behaving responsibly. He needs to know his actions have consequences," and my grandma laughs and shakes her head and says, "You really don't have a clue, do you?" and William says, "In many primitive cultures, 13 is the age at which a boy is initiated into manhood," and I say, "I'll be needing a spear, a blow gun, and a variety of poison darts."

My mom says, "A big group of friends... Roughhousing... Games... Presents...."

My grandma says, "Presents! Jimmy, put that mop down and come open your presents."

There are some presents in the middle of the table surrounded by a bunch of dirty dishes from the spaghetti dinner we just ate. I drop the mop and have a moment of weakness when I let my dad out of my sights because I'm distracted by the presents. I turn around and walk backward to the table, keeping my dad in my line of vision.

My dad cusses and picks up the mop and starts mopping the floor.

I open one present and it's books from my grandma—*Bigfoot LIVES!*, *The Truth About Roswell*, *Area 51 Exposed*. The books are old and smell like a basement which means they probably contain top-secret information that the government would execute me for having. Also, on the cover of *Area 51 Exposed*, the word *Exposed* is like an X-ray of the word *Exposed*, white on the inside and black on the outside, so you know it's the truth.

The other present from my grandma is two big Hershey bars. She says, "One for you and one for Charles." In case you never met Charles, he's a spider monkey and my best friend who no one in the world except me and my grandma believes is real.

My dad sighs and says, "Oh, great... Encourage him," and my grandma says, "Someone has to, and you're not up to the job," and my dad says, "I encourage him to be healthy," and my grandma says, "You encourage him to conform," and my mom says, "Open my present."

She hands me a present I know is a sweater before I open it because of the size and shape and because it's from my mom. I even know it will be dark blue so it won't violate my school dress code policy.

After I open it I act surprised and say, "Wow! Thanks, Mom" and give her a kiss and they should give me an Academy Award.

My dad hands me a package about half the size of a shoe box and I say, "I'll have to run this through radiology and poison control," and my grandma says, "I checked it out. It's clean."

I open the present and it's a shaving kit with a mug, brush, razor, and a bar of shaving soap all sealed in plastic.

My mom laughs, and says, "Richard, he doesn't need that!" and my dad says, "He will soon," and William says, "Indeed, the growth of facial hair begins with the initiation of puberty," and my dad says, "William, can we have a family moment without your commentary?"

I say, "How do I know the soap isn't acid? How do I know the razor won't cut my face off?" I start to throw the kit across the room, but my grandma stops me, and says, "I think it's safe. See? It's wrapped in plastic. Sealed by the factory. He couldn't tamper with it."

I hold it in my hands and stare at it. The mug has the words "Barbershop Quality" on it. The label says the brush is made of badger hair. Suddenly my face is hot and I'm sweating and the package seems to vibrate in my hands. I drop it on the table and step toward my mom.

"He doesn't need that," my mom says. She rubs my cheeks with her hands just to make sure.

The Michelin Man

Jesse Robinson

conceived in a marketer's mind
born from the womb of the rubber tree
the albino super hero lives
a man of stacked white rubber rolls multiplying
to tapered toes and head
a host of firm chubbiness undulating
to the nth degree cherubic cubed,
clean shaven porcelain
replete with brutish brawn
he is the antithesis of the juvenile over indulgence
and pudgy impulsivity of the Pillsbury Doughboy,
the Brawny Paper Towel Man
and Mr. Clean both caricatures of
bona fide bravery bow before his tactile presence
the embodiment of caution
his girth hugs the slender hips of streets
a living prophylactic, he is a ladies' man
ribbed for her pleasure his tread well worn
on lonely dark roads of roaming romance
groping pebbled black top
under the smoldering heat of internal combustion,
his guardianship impregnable
he remains a bachelor bound to safety
only relaxing at rest, rubbing down
his bulbous joints with Armor All, releasing his PSI
he loosens his steel belts preparing
for our next journey

To Norah, the Seeker

Cori Brown

Norah, the wind screams your name
Softly, as it sweeps across Loch Staonaig.
A Golden Dawn soaks the sky, Norah.
Alpha on your right, Omega on your left,
And the Devil in the dagger at your feet.

Norah, the darkened drape's icy chill
Covers the heightened hackles on your heart,
Christendom's Cross lies beneath you,
Across from the Abbey's Holy shore,
St. Columba wails on Iona, Norah.

Faeries' Mound ordained your deathly bed,
Norah, what demon folly have you made,
Lusting after the unknown and forbidden
You knew your evil lover hidden in haze
Awaited your silken bloody soul, Norah.

O, Pater Noster, pray save this ruined child,
Pawn of deception, glittering spangled Magick
Grows as a thornbush, piercing your heels,
Flee, flee, Norah, the saints surround your head,
And the heavens divide to find you, Norah.

I Found Jesus

Tyler Dunning

I FOUND BABY JESUS ABANDONED IN A grocery store dumpster yesterday. There were no tears, there was no crying. He'd screamed Himself calm amongst the refuse; the mother wasn't coming back. And it was only by arbitrarily throwing a Snickers wrapper in the trash that I saw the twitching bare flesh, dirty and soiled like a diaper. He was discovered.

My heart murmured a shameful response: to keep walking, to pretend I'd seen nothing. Like the time I caught Aaron smelling clothes left in the fitting rooms at work—head down, kept walking. But this was somehow different, not only because of the innocence and divinity, but because I knew what it was to be abandoned. I too had been left. Twice, actually.

First, I was abandoned by fairness: I hadn't become my parent's only child by birth, but by terminal cancer. Watching my older brother, who was just old enough to legally drink, slowly submit to his fate became a lesson in extreme sympathy—his loss of appetite was mine, his sleepless nights kept me awake, his chemo treatments sapped my energy. By the end, the brother I once knew was reduced to unsteady breathing, considerate smiles to those displaying more fear than him, and a limited mobility to that of a hospital bed. But even in death he never left me, and me never him. What was lost, however, was the notion that this world was somehow just, because to believe good things happened to good people would mean my brother somehow failed the basic parameters of this equation. And I wasn't willing to make that compromise.

The second thing to abandon me was enchantment: as a child I believed the hype of a happily-ever-after. But I was born to a false kingdom: my parents owned and operated a used book store—a store which once flourished before the advent of the Internet and online book sales, but soon became a tomb for simpler times. And, like the bookstore, my parent's once-romantic relationship suffered under the weight of unfortunate reality: accumulating hospital bills and the inconsolable sorrow of losing a child.

The divorce was sudden but not unexpected.

My mother kept the house, eventually filling any floor space or empty countertop with the hundreds of books we couldn't sell when the store went under. She would rearrange them endlessly. My father moved north to endure a harsher winter. They were both punishing themselves in different ways, trying to avoid the haunt of a failed family.

Living with my mother, I would spend my darker days skimming the pages of the literary rejects, often wondering how different my reading choices would be had the genres of disease and divorce not been introduced to me. My idea of heroics became quietly dealing with clinical depression, something far less gallant than I had imagined for my life. Courage became avoiding any situation requiring emotional investment. I squandered talent on dead-end jobs, squandered relationships on anything but commitment. Enchantment, with all the dragons and damsels, was a story I no longer subscribed to.

So looking at Jesus, now abandoned in a dumpster, I empathized with the little guy. I just kept staring as the grocery bags started weighing heavy in my once-muscular arms. I never thought I'd find Him here, especially while doing such a routine chore. I was just there to retrieve my weekly staple items: a loaf of the cheapest white bread, one dozen eggs, two percent milk. My life was simple and unhealthy, my meals recurring. I couldn't have this interrupted. A baby would radically change things.

Libby, my current girlfriend, wanted a baby more than anything. We talked about kids occasionally. I always feigned interest, saying I would love to have a family but making sure to never actually use the word children. She saw through this though.

She saw right through me.

If she believed she had any other options she would have left, but something had abandoned her too: a notion of self-worth. This was accompanied by weight gain and poor posture—she used to be so beautiful.

But the truth is I'd never actually felt the paternal urge to have a child; in fact, I felt shocking resistance to the idea, at least in comparison to the people around me. My brother used to ramble on about coaching his kids one day, how there would be a baseball diamond in their backyard. He relished the idea of tormenting any suitor trying to date the daughter he might eventually have. But for me, I feared these responsibilities. I feared seeing my kids hurt, worrying they'd consider the world just as bleak as I did.

So to find a wallowing baby in a dumpster was terrifying, not just because of the inhumanity, but because of the reality it made me face: sometimes things are lost unnecessarily just as they are sometimes found.

I ran through all the scenarios in my head: hiding behind a car and waiting to see if some other passerby would take the child, calling the police and letting professionals handle the situation, or shamefully leaving as I had originally thought to do. But none of this was feasible because I knew what was required of me—I believed it was a sign to find this savior at the local Albertsons, and I guess I wanted to be a savior for saving this renowned savior in such a way.

I slowly lifted Him out of the trash.

"Shit..." I whispered to myself as I walked unconfidently back into the grocery store, now lugging a half-naked baby over my right hip. Nobody mentioned anything about my revisit to the store; nobody mentioned the dingy condition of the child I now mysteriously possessed. On the contrary, as I bought formula and diapers, the cashier commented on the cuteness of Jesus. I felt a swell of undeserved pride. I thanked her.

I loaded everything into the backseat of my rundown Saab—everything except Jesus. I was already having second thoughts. The metal manger of which I found Him was right there, 50 feet away. I could end this just as quickly as it started, placing the baby back in the trash. But I wanted to feel alive again. I wanted to break this cycle of lackluster living. Mostly I just wanted Libby to love me again. And none of this was going to happen without significant change.

Jesus brought change. I knew this because it wasn't my first time finding Him—it certainly wasn't my most irresponsible reaction to the matter either.

§

The first time I found Jesus was at a little league baseball tournament. I wasn't playing; I was reluctantly there to watch my brother. This was before his bones started aching. This was before I'd rub his back while he retched hopelessly over the toilet. No, these were the healthy days, back when I was eight, hated sports, and was only interested in *Star Wars*.

It was by chance or happenstance that I found Jesus there. His brother was also playing in the tournament on an opposing team from a distant land. Both of us being around the same age, we were immediately drawn to each other's company.

It started with awkward glances across the poorly-painted bleachers. Thinking back, I remember Him being from an ethnic family, most likely Puerto Rican—their English staccato but understandable. His parents continually referred to Him as Santiago, but years later I came to realize the truth. A deity can go by many names, many appearances—this one with tattered clothes draped over olive skin.

At the time, I didn't really know what faith was. I guess I still don't. My family was the type of secular that didn't find religion important enough to even consider. All I knew was people carried a lightness within, as if the words of sacred texts were twisted through their grain, like a knot in a tree, to make the pious a little more profane.

Growing up I paid no attention to the institution of religion—well not until I began spending so much time in prayer. This was at a period when I should've been recklessly sinning through teenage plight. Instead I was praying for the health of others, praying for an understanding of this 'better place' we all supposedly go. Praying eventually gave way to pleading, which eventually gave way to silent anger.

This is all to say, at the time of the baseball tournament I didn't even notice Jesus's divinity. I noticed his toys. He was playing with broken model trucks in the dirt; I casually invited myself into the situation. The first thing He said, as He smashed two trucks together, was: "What if every day was dangerous?" I picked up the largest truck and rammed it directly into both of His, responding: "I don't know."

After interacting in this manner for what seemed like hours (the boredom of baseball didn't bend time for the better), we decided to explore the perils of the nearby playground. There were trees, monkey bars, winding slides—there was adventure. We slid the slides. We monkeyed around. Then we found a tree upon which all other trees should be measured. This tree, most likely a pine, reached to the heavens—branches extended like arms in hysterical prayer. Jesus dared me to climb it. I refused, lying that I'd climbed it before and was bored with the prospect. I was actually just terrified of the height. I challenged Him to climb it instead.

Coyly, He accepted the offer and approached the tree. I gave Him a boost to the first branch and wished Him luck. He tore His already torn clothes. He caught sap in His unwashed hair. He showed no reservations; the strange little boy just kept climbing and climbing. I could tell He was starting to get nervous about halfway up—a fall would've killed him... again. But He kept going. He didn't want to disappoint me.

Approaching the top, I could hear Jesus calling down to me. It seemed like He was miles above the earth's surface. His message was muted; I could barely make out what He was saying. I got the impression He needed help though. I instantly panicked, thinking I could never climb such a grand tree, that I could never rise to such great heights. I started crying uncontrollably. And in my mind crying wasn't a dignified condition for anyone wanting to be a toy smasher or a lying tree climber, so instead of getting help I hid. I hid in the back of my parent's bullet-shaped minivan. I was there until the game ended and we left. I never told anyone Jesus was stuck in the tree, and I never saw that version of Him again.

§

"You alright back there?" I asked, driving the three blocks from Albertsons to my apartment complex. "Ya know, I used to walk. That was some years ago... but I'm eventually gonna lose this weight. I wrestled in high school—145 pounds of lean muscle. Man, was I in shape back then. I lost it all when I quit the team, once my brother got sick... anyway... I don't even wanna to tell you what I weigh now. Libby gives me grief about it. I think you'll get along with her... not that you're giving me a hard time, it's just, she's really great with kids, that's all." Jesus wasn't responding, not even a whimper, but I kept rambling nervously as I circled the block, time after time, waiting for the closest parking spot to open. I didn't want to be seen in public with Him—neighbors would have questions.

Once parked, I found Jesus fast asleep amongst the groceries. I awkwardly, but delicately, cradled Him in the nook of my elbow as I lumbered everything into my one-room studio. I set the bags on the floor and quickly started clearing junk off my coffee table: half-read books, unpaid bills, cigarette butts. I shifted Jesus from my arm to the freshly vacant spot. Looking at Him slumber, I whispered, "Now what?"

I wanted to tell Him everything. I wanted to tell Him about my parents and how they wouldn't be visiting much, not because of a loss of love, but because they were so wrapped up in the busy business of trying to forgive the past. I wanted to tell Him about Libby and how, when I first met her, actually thought she was the Buddha. It was the way she carried nothingness in her heart, existing free of all attachments and desires. The way she shined when she walked into a room, as if enlightenment emanated from her pores.

I wanted to tell Jesus everything, but I didn't say a word. I just let Him sleep as I cleaned my apartment for the first time in months.

The first few days with Jesus were fine, and I knew I'd made the right decision. He slept most of the time, and when awake I gave Him formula, which seemed to work. I let Him have my bed at night, building a pillow fortress around the parameter of the mattress. I slept on the floor, occasionally waking up to make sure He was still breathing.

The fourth day proved a little more difficult—difficult not because of the child, per say, but because of the interrupted rituals a child brings. It was Sunday, a day I normally spent watching football at the local bar with my friends. When I didn't show up, I received harassing text messages. I ignored them all.

The only text I sent that day was to Libby and it was a lie. It read: *Haven't heard from you in a while... but I have the flu so you should probably stay clear for a few days*. Her response was typical and annoying: *K*.

She made no attempts at delivering soup.

I still hadn't told her about the baby. Despite all my initial gusto, I feared how she'd react. I mean, how do you really tell someone you found Jesus in a dumpster? Or at a little league baseball game? There was a lot I hadn't told her, like my prolonged experimentation with ecstasy, or why I actually had an Alaska tattoo on my forearm. I never told her about the second time I found Jesus.

§

The second time I found Jesus was nearly twenty years after the baseball tournament. This time He was a charismatic frat boy from upstate New York, the kind spoiled by business-professional parents His whole life: private schools and ivy leagues, exotic trips during seasonal vacations. I first spotted Him dancing drunk on a table in Prague. I was in Europe backpacking with a former girlfriend, the one before Libby. It was supposed to be a romantic getaway, but we fought tirelessly—I think Jesus saw this as an opportunity to seduce her by first covertly befriending me.

I initially didn't want anything to do with Him; I saw Him as just another Euro-trashed rich kid who drank shamelessly, experimented with party drugs, and used distant lands to recreate Lord-of-the-Flies scenarios. But the more time I spent with Him and the more inebriated I got, I realized, yet again, that Jesus was somehow different from the rest and absurdly appealing. At one point, while dancing on the table with Him, He said, "What is the only sacred space left in the world?"

Unable to really focus on the question, I turned to vomit from our pulpit and nearly fell off in the act. Cleaning my face in an inefficient manner, I finally responded, "I don't know."

"Public restrooms," He chuckled, as His eyes mirrored the movements of a passing girl. I was too distracted to ask why, or maybe I just don't remember the reasoning. Either way, we danced the ecstasy from our blood and somehow ended up in an alley with two underage Algerians who were demonstrating how to pickpocket tourists. After spending what seemed like hours (the delirium of drugs always bent time for the best) in the unassuming alley, Jesus and I decided to find our way back to a pizza place we'd passed with mesmerizing flashing lights—we were craving fatty food and cheap entertainment. Along the way I swear he was performing miracles; I muttered: "Why didn't you do anything?"

"Huh?"

"You didn't save him... ya just let him die."

He shook his head, confused, "Here, take this." He held out a small plastic bag. Wetting my finger, I put my pinky in the offering. A film of white powder, I put the finger back in my mouth.

The rest of the drug-induced journey was a bit of a blur, but there are two things I know for certain and one thing I only suspect: I know Jesus and I got matching tattoos of Alaska on our forearms, I know Jesus pickpocketed my wallet, and I suspect Jesus slept with my girlfriend that night. He was gone by the time I woke up and all I had to remember Him by was a stolen identity, a poorly drawn tattoo, and a future ex-girlfriend... well, that was until I found Him years later in the dumpster.

§

The sixth day with the baby was my nightmare: there was perpetual shit in His diaper, He wouldn't stop wailing despite my best efforts, there was no free time to do anything. I was forced to recognize I couldn't sustain the child on ramen noodles, expired milk, and anime films. I even gathered the courage to walk Him around the neighborhood, but all that came from it was strangers wanting to discuss the miracle of life. They would ask the age of Jesus, the answer of which I was completely oblivious. If I told them six months they would look at me confused; if I told them a year they would react in amazement. I decided to stick with the latter.

That night I laid on the hard wood floor with a pillow smothering my face as Jesus screamed on the bed. I screamed into the pillow in retaliation, muted words of abject frustration: *I don't even believe in you.*

I couldn't believe the predicament I was in: a once promising life wasted on the comfort of never taking risks, parents fading with the loss of one son at the expense of another, and a girlfriend who deserved nothing but better. And now this—Jesus. This was maybe my last chance at salvation and I had no idea what to do. All I heard was the static screaming.

By 2 a.m., when nothing had changed, I loaded Jesus into my car. In lieu of a child safety seat I used blankets and pillows. We drove across town to Libby's apartment and parked outside her window. She had moved here to be with me, 1,243 miles, and still I couldn't fully commit, convincing her it would be better if we lived separately. Jesus and I sat there for about an hour, Him whimpering and me staring into the darkness of a bedroom—the closest thing to love I would probably ever have. I thought about leaving a note, but I really had nothing to say.

Our second stop was the cemetery. A gate blocked the entrance, as it was beyond visiting hours. I simply ducked under it as I always had—this time with Jesus on my hip. We weaved in and out of graves, making our way to the southwest corner. We dodged shrubs and trees in the darkness, a memorized landscape that only a reoccurring visitor could navigate. This is where I would escape my parent's constant bickering, where I would come to feel less lonely on the holidays.

Standing over my brother's grave with Jesus, I said: "I don't remember his laugh. I don't remember the details of his face. I don't even remember the inside jokes. My pictures of him only offer a simplified version... but he's more than that, my memories have to run deeper than that... I just don't remember why... I guess everything can't be saved despite my best intentions."

By 4 a.m., we were right back where it all started: the grocery store. I apologized for deserting Him in the tree and told Him not to worry about my stolen wallet. I also apologized for what I was about to do—for abandoning Him in a dumpster. But I think we both knew it would be better if someone else found Him, someone that could actually take care of Him. He didn't fuss or put up a fight as I lowered Him into the trash. Miraculously, He was finally calm again.

§

A couple years have passed since the last time I found Jesus. Not much has changed, and He only comes to mind occasionally. But when He does, I think about those six days and how I never did confess what I planned on naming Him: Michael, just like my brother.

Black and White:

A Color Memory, 1944 (Or, Why I Never Learned to Play the Piano)

Sylvia Levinson

"Whoa, Bessie," my dad calls out to the big Palomino
plow horse. The girl, me, six-years old, short brown hair, faded
overalls, barefoot and bareback astride Bessie. My legs dangle
not even halfway down the mare's wide side. I hold her soft mane,
smile into the camera. A man, tall and thin, stringy black hair,
sunken cheeks, also in overalls and a John Deere cap, grips
the halter rope. He is not smiling.

My sister and I are sorting through a box of snapshots, faded
and cracked from 60 years of careless storage. *Do you
remember him?* I ask. *Yes. Frank, the hired man. He dropped
his pants in front of us once. He did? I don't remember. Where?
In the stairway behind the kitchen—you know, that place
you hid when I cut your leg with the sickle.*

The scar on my left shin marks the cutting accident and I can see
me hiding from our nervous mom in the backstairs, stanching blood
with an old washcloth. No memory of the pants incident, but this one
comes: I'm nine—the yellow-toothed piano teacher, his greasy gray
hair, smell of mothballs and secrets on his worn corduroy jacket, he
sits too close to me on the bench, grips my fingers too tightly, shows
me where to place them.

Breath (Ruach)

Sylvia Levinson

your convex chest
bird breast
all keel bone
rises falls holds
open-mouthed
gasps remembering
how

you entered
this world shocked
into first suck of air
your tiny inflatables
forced out fluid
tested their untried bellows
nine months inert your
mother breathed you
now

750 million a lifetime
of breaths close
to the end fluids again
fill your weary lungs
bird sips of bottled oxygen
you await the long exhale

Miss Lake Geneva

Megan Elliott

F ROM THE WEST END OF THE grandstand you could see the ocean, the
Pacific shimmering and buckling in the late afternoon sun. I stood on
the balcony with a cigarette, watching an old man who sat on a nearby bench.
He was a nervous cluster of small, twitchy movements, chain-smoking while
he read the *Daily Racing Form*. His foot tapped in time to no music at all
and when his free, ink-stained hand was not turning the paper's page, he
alternated between chewing his yellowed fingernails and gnawing on the end
of a Bic ballpoint. Occasionally, he'd circle something, and I could see from
the way he gripped his pen that he was pressing hard on the newsprint.

I dropped my cigarette in an ashtray and walked over to him.

"Who do you like in seven?"

The man turned his face toward me. He licked his lips as he looked me
up and down, narrowing his watery blue eyes. I narrowed my eyes right back
at him.

"Fuck off," he said.

"I just wanted a tip." I shrugged my shoulders and turned to go.

"You're not a real gambler," the man called after me. "You're just a tourist."

The glass door to the smoking porch swung shut behind me. I walked
toward the bar and bought an over-priced beer. The bartender overfilled the
plastic cup, and foam ran over the lip and between my fingers. I sipped a
quarter inch of the beer and then walked slowly back to my seat, with careful,
deliberate steps, taking care not to spill. I maneuvered with the same focus
I had when I was a child and would walk circles around the dining room
table with a book balanced on my head. One foot in front of the other, the
surrounding world falling away behind me.

Back in the stands, I took a seat next to Phillip. His shoulders were
hunched, and his thin, bony hands rested on the back of the seat in front of
him as he read the racing program that lay in his lap. When he turned toward
me, his dark hair fell across his dark eyes. On the night I'd fallen in love with

him his hair had looked exactly the same, and for a moment my heart lit up again like it had at that party, just before he'd leaned in to kiss me.

"You didn't get me a beer?"

I took another long swallow of the Coors Light, which tasted like it had come from a keg in a dirty Midwestern basement, and said nothing.

Phillip frowned. Silence made him restless. "What do you think of Number eight?"

I looked at the screen and saw the horses circling in the paddock. The horse in question was the deep gray of an approaching summer thunderstorm cloud, one that would come in with fury and leave with cleansing suddenness. He cantered around the dirt circle, head held high. Confident.

"What's its name?"

"You know the name doesn't matter. It's completely irrelevant."

I pulled the racing program out of my purse and flipped to the page for the seventh race. My eyes scanned the list and settled on Number eight: Dexysmidniterunner. It wasn't a good name.

"I don't like it."

He rolled his eyes. "What's wrong with it?"

"I hate that song."

"What song do you hate?"

"Come on Eileen."

"What's wrong with you? Everyone loves that song."

"Not me. How much did you wager?"

"Fifty bucks."

I shrugged. "It's your loss."

Phillip rolled his eyes and turned his attention back to the board. I sipped my beer and looked over the names of the other horses in this race. "Helen of Troy," "Dark and Stormy," "My Girl." I settled on "Miss Lake Geneva" and got up to make my bet. I had a good feeling about this one.

I waited in behind a woman wearing lucite heels and a dress that clung to her curves like a bandage. The man standing next to her wore a fedora and his hand kept drifting down to her ass, and every once in a while she'd swat at it like you might a mosquito.

At the window, I put down my cash—$200 to win—and took my voucher. Back in the stands, I found Phillip looking over the list of horses for the next race.

"Why don't you wait to see who wins this one first?"

"I want to be prepared."

I frowned. Phillip wanted to be prepared for everything, and as a result, was rarely prepared for anything. When we first started dating, he told me that he sometimes lay awake at night and thought about how he would escape if his apartment was engulfed in flames. I told him that once, when I lived in Milwaukee, an apartment down the hall from me had caught on fire, and I'd woken up in the middle of the night to screeching sound of a smoke detector and the pounding feet of firemen.

"What did you do?" Phillip asked.

"I walked out the front door," I said. "It wasn't a big deal."

"What a nightmare," he said.

"Not really," I replied.

We waited for the race to start, not talking. Phillip folded the racing program, unfolded it, then folded it again. I sipped my beer, which had gone warm and flat in the summer heat. It was five minutes after five.

The horses emerged, one by one, from under the grandstand and made their way to the starting gate. Dexysmidniterunner was in the front, regal and assured. Miss Lake Geneva was number ten, the last to emerge. Her tail twitched as she pulled against her pony. When she got to the gate, she balked, and I thought for a moment she might scratch, but she finally relaxed, and the gate closed behind her.

I held my breath. In the moment before a race began, it seemed like all things were possible.

"And away they go!" The announcer cried as the horses sprang from their cages. Phillip stood up, his hand gripping the seat in front of him so tight that his knuckles turned white. Neither of our horses was in front. Number eight was running solid in the middle of the pack. My horse stumbled out of the gate and started far back, too far back, I guessed, to catch up.

The horses rounded the curve on the west end of the track. To my surprise, Miss Lake Geneva pulled out of last place. My eyes flicked between the screen, where jerky, pixelated horses ran, and the track itself, which was a blur of color and hooves. Number ten was no longer in second-to-last place, leaping forward to sixth, then fourth. The race would be over soon. The horses in the lead had fallen back. Number ten and Number eight were neck and neck now, with just one horse in front of them. I did not look at Phillip, and he did not look at me. We kept our eyes locked on the track.

Then Number eight was no longer running. The horse went down in an awkward, painful tumble, throwing his rider from the saddle. The other horses broke around them, pounding on down the track. The jockey lay, his legs twisted, face down in the turf. A medical crew raced to the scene. By the time I looked away, the race was over. Miss Lake Geneva had finished first.

I did not want to think about what would happen to the other horse.

Phillip's face had gone slack. His mouth opened and closed, opened and closed, but no sound came out. I reached over and touched his hand.

"I'm sorry."

He pulled away. When he turned to look at me, his eyes were narrow and dark.

"Why don't you go gloat somewhere else?"

"I'm not gloating." I needed money to leave, to buy a plane ticket back to Chicago and to start again, and so I had wanted to win. But I hadn't wanted it to happen like this.

Phillip pulled away. His other hand was balled into a tight, small fist, the crumpled edges of his voucher peeking through between his thumb and forefinger. Slowly he unrolled his fingers. He tore the paper into tiny pieces, which fluttered down to the sticky cement like snow.

We sat for a few moments more. The ambulance carrying the jockey had gone, and some men were loading the injured horse into a truck. My heart felt like it would break.

"What do you want me to do?"

Phillip looked at the ground and did not reply. I didn't love him anymore but it still hurt to see him like this.

"I can stay," I said. "I'll stay if you want me to. Just ask."

"I don't want you to stay. I want you to be happy."

He both did and did not want me to be happy. My happiness was fine only if I could achieve it without taking some of his in the process. He was selfish, but then so was I.

"Leaving will make me happy," I said. Phillip lifted his eyes to meet mine.

"You're really going to do this," he said. "For certain this time?"

I nodded. I was not sad, yet somehow I still felt myself swallowing hard to avoid the tears.

"Well you better get out of here then."

"I'm sorry," I said again. "I'm sorry about the horse."

He shrugged. "There will be other horses." He tried to sound stoic.

I leaned over to kiss him on the cheek. "Goodbye," I said, my lips close to his ear. He grabbed my arm tight, his fingers pushing into the skin hard enough to bruise, and then let go.

"Goodbye," he said.

I left Phillip in the stands, mourning his loss. After I cashed my voucher and slid those crisp bills into my purse, I walked out of the racetrack and turned my back to the setting sun. I was ready to go home.

The River Rising

Judy Reeves

IT WAS A SPRING DAY, APRIL, maybe on a Tuesday, when the river lifted its big brown back like a rhinoceros and spread out over the land. Wide, muddy water lapping up fields and farms and livestock. Cattle standing dumb on their four locked feet while the water rose up their legs. Chickens fluttered their feathers as if their wings could carry them above it all, and clutched onto whatever cottonwood or willow branch would hold them, while below the water spread its chocolate stain, slurping up homes, barns, outhouses, the chicken's coops.

There goes the crop—corn stalks that just got their green legs, and the wheat and the soybeans and the early gardens and Mrs. Peavey's prize peonies and the roses she planted when her son came home from the war.

Twelve feet past flood stage and rising still and tractors and baling machines and pickup trucks and cars and yellow school busses swallowed down in thirsty gulps. Farmers cursing and their wives wailing and children thinking it's all a grand piece of excitement and the poor dogs that drowned and the man trying to save his cow and the old woman on her roof, clinging to the chimney singing *What a friend we have in Jesus.*

All around the news crews with their flash bulbs and microphones and radio reporters talking into tape recorders and preachers praying and someone has a tambourine.

The river's taking back her bed, carving out a new flow where the highway used to run with its yellow lines and Burma Shave signs and edges that fell away to dusty ditches.

Nobody knows how far and wide she'll go before she's done. We shake our heads, do what we can. Stand at her edge tossing sandbags like pillows on her bed.

Thou Shalt Steal Only This

Shannon Bates

O UR PARENTS NEVER WAVERED ON THE topic of ethics. We didn't need religion to know that morality is very important. We would never kill anyone. There was no question. We would treat others with the respect we ourselves deserved. But there was one small allowance our father made when it came to stealing, and for this, he required our participation.

We saw many cars pull in and out of our driveway over the years, and these were definitely purchased. They didn't cost much—old clunkers our dad called "classics," tiny sedans that barely squeezed all five of us in if I sat on the hump between my sister and brother in the middle of the backseat, and a couple of vans. The vans were the most fun, of course. They were great for hauling entire soccer or baseball teams from place to place without needing (in those days) to worry about a seatbelt or even a seat for each child. I preferred to sit on the floor of the cavernous white beast we had for a while. I enjoyed the tickle of the fantastic blue shag against the backs of my calves. That van certainly took a beating. My brother's teammates nearly toppled it by rocking it back and forth from the inside while waiting in the parking lot before heading to a tournament. I turned a full cartwheel in the sliding door runner with tennis balls in my hands when our dad stopped fast once on a family trip. The rear chairs swiveled like Star Trek command stations, and the very back of the vehicle was often a bed for a child or pet.

I can still hear the solid *thunk* of the dangerous sliding door on that van. It's a wonder we didn't lose anyone while piling dozens of teammates or roller skating children in the back within seconds on hundreds of trips. But that door was very useful when it came to our father's guilty pleasure.

"Hold on," he'd warn, "not yet."

My brother or sister would have a hand on the door lever, waiting for Dad's cue. The other would squat where the door opens and watch for the signal. Being the smallest and the least useful in these situations, I would sit on the carpeted half circle of the wheel well with my hands on my knees. The van would slow substantially but never reach a full stop.

"Now!" I could see the thrill in Dad's eyes in the rearview mirror.

The van door would slide open and my brother or sister would lean out just enough to retrieve the prize before our dad sped up again and the door slammed shut.

Traffic cones and pylons were fascinating to me. Their rubbery, tough forms allowed for all sorts of contortions. I liked to wear the cones as hats, or use them as megaphones. A pylon, once a ball was placed atop its tower, was a perfect tee for batting practice. A cone was a great substitute for a motionless opponent in soccer, although our dad really did like using trash cans, if only to embarrass us when he announced that the trash cans had won the match. We collected many of these orange treasures over the years, and they were put to great use in our backyard and on the playing fields.

To this day, when I see a hazard zone on the road, I have to keep myself from slowing down and leaning out my door to grab the cones for Dad. I wonder if he does the same.

At Recess

Brian Thedell

I'm spun. You can imagine a spinning top
—if you'd like—but of course I'm talking about speed,
two time-release Ritalin that I took this morning
before your visit
because I wanted to see, clearly;
because I wanted to see, sharply;
I wanted to pull out the great big crayon box
of myself, to find the brightest color—
I wanted to draw myself in thick, heavy lines,
I wanted bits of my wax to flake off the page...

And you bring all of space with you,
from the rolling lawn off my second story window,
when you're here, you draw out
the lines I color within; your words form
the soaked-in tracing that I fill with all my wild hues...

And in its way, friendship is more delicate
than romance; there is no buffer of body, of skin
to separate its closeness. The time we spend together
quickens, thickens, like the time between recess bells
when purpose and play break with an urgency
only children can appreciate—well, children and us...

Here, in this space, everything you are
means something, everything we say is important,
and there in between us I am
every color, I am every line.

So here I am, spinning in space. Here I am, spinning
in time, spinning until a final clang rings out across the
playground. Come visit, bring your dodgeball, your
colored chalk, your brand new Megatron action figure.
But don't lean in too close because, after all,
you just might tip me over...

My Mother and the Sunday Meal

America Salvatore

begins with a prayer of martyrdom, a scent of
    Shalimar mixed with garlic. My mother
conducts a conversation with a whirl to her
    voice, hoping the rest of us will follow her
    lead.
A crucifix above the stove, the doll collection
    praying for passage. Empty glasses stand
at attention in the breakfront. Furniture
    suffocates under plastic, her honesty in
    how my
sister's latest hair color makes her eyes squint.
    The radio is the only other voice that
dares to speak. Until my father peers up from
    his newspaper, barks why the songs
now-a-days repeat the same line over and over.
    And my mother in her most devouring
voice utters *pass the butter, pass the butter*.

January

America Salvatore

I should correct January for perfect timing,
year after year doing what it must.
I know my grief has a chance to be
covered under the ceiling of urban flakes.
Cold wind breathes
through me and stings my throat
threatening my chance to tell lies.
Just let the winter show its face.
I will show it what to do.
But I am untrustworthy.
January is a master of contrast,
red blood and white snow,
always ready for new challenges.
As for me, I'll move about January
like a cat and sleep and wait,
no leaps, no squeals.
I'll gaze, only as I can.

Night Takes the Queen

Andrew Printer

It wasn't until we were through customs and immigration, past baggage claim and well beyond the edge of the airport that I emerged from my silent, numb nothing. I blinked and Texas sprang into dimension with the crazy-fake proportions of a pop-up book: a slip of freeway buckled up and over my head then swept away toward a smear of dirt-scrabble beige. To my left a dirty cactus reached for the sky. On a billboard to my right cattle grazed. And in the distance Dallas spiked the sky like the castles of Oz, so many towers of sparkly glass.

All of everything was big and unreal.

I blinked again and it was clear I was in a comic book land, dropped into a wood-paneled station wagon bouncing through a slice of American dust. Not just me but my mother too, and my sisters Holly and Jane. We were four bleary-eyed faces gazing at strange.

Lacey Blackburn was behind the wheel of the car, the seat beside her stacked up shoulder-high with some of our suitcases, the ones that wouldn't fit into the long flat back of her car. Mrs. Blackburn picked us up at the airport and boy did she talk. I don't remember her talking quite so much back in Hong Kong. She and her husband Chad were always so movie-star cool, both of them as modern and American as a couple could be. Mrs. Blackburn always wore cat's eye-shaped sunglasses, day and night, thick black lenses with dark gray frames. Mr. Blackburn looked too old for her, too craggy-faced and serious to have three kids smaller than me. But then Lacey wasn't his first wife. She wasn't even his third.

"Everyone's excited to see you guys!" Mrs. Blackburn shouted over her shoulder, over the roar of the fast moving traffic.

We were in the backseat. All four of us sat in a row. The windows of the station wagon were part way down so we were five heads of hair flapping in a hot dry wind. I sat next to the passenger side door, an urgent thumb scratching the inside of my fist. Holly and Jane were squeezed in the middle,

Holly, two years younger than me but about the same size squashed right up against me. Two year-old Jane lay drooped across my mother's lap.

"Pam and Cole are waiting at home," Mrs. Blackburn told us. "Kim's at gymnastics camp. She'll see you tomorrow."

Mrs. Blackburn talked with an unfamiliar enthusiasm, an odd upbeat urgency. She sounded too happy, her honey soft twang too eager to make everything sound like a promise.

"Chad's away too," she told us. "He's in Denver for business. But he'll be back by the weekend. I thought we'd go to Six Flags on Sunday. It's like Disneyland, but smaller, no Mickey Mouse, just rides. You kids like roller-coasters, right?"

"We haven't been on a roller-coaster before," Holly said. Her bright English voice sounded so small and polite piping up next to Mrs. Blackburn's booming lilt.

"You haven't been on a roller-coaster!" Mrs. Blackburn positively screamed her surprise. "Well, we'll have to fix that real fast."

Jane's large dark eyes popped open and she began to cry one of her short dry complaints. She stopped as soon as she started, lifted herself up then dropped back against my mother's arm where she fell back asleep.

Was everyone in Texas going to be this enthusiastic, I wondered? Maybe this is how Americans talk when they're in America, instead of some faraway place like Hong Kong where they can slink about, being foreign? I didn't like it. Mrs. Blackburn's excitement made me feel obligated, like I had to match her happiness smile for smile, laugh for laugh.

I looked at Jane and watched a bubble of dribble pool on her lip. It wobbled with the bounce of the car threatening to spill down her chin. Holly was wrong I thought. We have been on a roller-coaster before. We're on one now.

Then I understood, just like that, just like one of those silly light bulbs that blink on above a comic book head. Mrs. Blackburn hadn't turned into a loud American. My dad was dead. Mrs. Blackburn was doing what every grown up had been doing since him and his car were cut in two by a bus on a dark wet road just six months ago. Only she was being louder about it, not as tip-toe proper as other adults up until now.

She was trying to make it okay.

The Blackburns' were my parents' friends. They lived on the Kowloon side of Hong Kong in a fancy apartment building popular with American businessmen, suit and tie people who carried themselves crisp and tight. The family had been part of our lives forever. There's a photo of Mrs. Blackburn in our family photo album. She's sitting on the sand in the sun-shiny glow of a bright striped awning. She's wearing a red bathing suit, hugging her knees tight to her chest, looking at three year old me in the foreground through her squinty cat's eye frames. She's not angry, not happy—just a self-serious movie star blank that I can't figure out. I'm standing fully naked before her, my plump baby bottom preserved forever on film.

The whole Blackburn family, all five of them, visited us at our house in Repulse Bay a few times a year. They were one of many couples with yellow-haired kids who came and swam and went away more golden than when they arrived.

Then they were gone altogether.

Moved to Dallas.

And now, so had we.

"It's for the best," Mrs. Blackburn said, twisting away from the road, trying to make eye-contact with my mother in the seat behind her. "At least for a while. You made the right decision."

"I couldn't stay in London," my mother shouted back, leaning forward, straining to compete with the wind. "It was impossible." Her voice was hoarse from smoking, crying, talking. There had been so much of all three since the accident. The few months we had just spent in England between Hong Kong and now had transformed her. Living with her parents, my grandparents, made her unrecognizable. Bit by bit the mother I knew dissolved into their daughter then re-formed as another mother, my mother once removed. Gone was the exotic woman with serene cross-legged poise, the cut-glass conductor of all things domestic. Here now in her place was an erratic, puffy-eyed person, someone wet with excess emotion, not sadness really, something more desperate than that, something unstable.

The car lurched, launching me into the air an inch or two then back down onto the sharp edge of a buckle. I twisted myself so that my back was flat against the door, away from the handles and knobs and the low slung city rushing by. I wasn't interested in Texas. I was interested in my mother. I studied her, my finger still scraping the inside of my wadded up hand. She was straining forward, almost bowing before Mrs. Blackburn, her face above an ashtray built into the armrest. She and Mrs. Blackburn were barking short sentences at each other over the wind, practicalities about sleeping arrangements, money and food. My mother's tan was pale and poached in the car's sad afternoon light, her flesh somehow thicker. The wind was blowing her hair flat against her head. She looked aged, oddly bald.

I had begun watching my mother soon after the accident. At first I wasn't watching, I was looking, hoping to catch her eye so that my eyes could tell her that I had something to say. But she never looked back, not really. In time I felt my gaze drain of purpose. Then my eyes just stopped looking altogether, so I watched.

She and I didn't speak either, not about my dad being gone, not about anything that mattered, nothing quiet or real. At my grandparents' house every bit of energy—and there was a lot of it, most of it loud and shockingly mean sizzled and spat between my mother and her parents. Aunts and uncles paid us kind attention, but my mother didn't. The only words directed at me or Holly were routine scolds that veered toward the scary edge of impatience.

I stayed nearby anyway, drew closer in fact. I was the only boy and the oldest so I was used to hearing my name being called all the time. Stephen this, Stephen that. Help your mother with her bags, help with Jane. I kept near enough so that my name only had to be called once.

I couldn't bear the idea that my mother might disintegrate. Small spiky panics erupted inside me at the thought of her not being who she always was. I couldn't imagine her not held together, slim, china-quiet and beautiful. The prospect of her falling to pieces and staying that way picked at a fearful part of me. I knew that beneath my mother's crisp exterior was something unpredictable, someone fragile. I think I'd known this forever. I figured that if I kept close enough I could help her with the little things and help hold her together, or at least help keep her looking that way. I made it my job to keep her shiny and whole. She didn't ask me to do this. Instinct urged me on, an anxious part of me that knew to stay tethered, for her sake and mine.

I stared at the smear of hair blowing flat against her head and I felt sorry for her. I was irritated that she had to compromise herself, sit doubled over in the back of a kid-sticky car with specks of cigarette ash flying in her face. She and Mrs. Blackburn stopped talking and my mother relaxed back into her seat. She blew her nose into a soggy tissue lodged in her hand.

"Are we crazy to be here?" she asked no one in particular. "Maybe we should have stayed."

§

I looked at the side of Mrs. Blackburn's face and it occurred to me that she was wearing a new, different pair of sunglasses. This new pair had bigger lenses than before. They were browner, rounder, like those worn by the Chinese girls who ran wild on the beach back in Hong Kong.

The car's indicator began clicking, nipping my train of thought. We approached an intersection and Mrs. Blackburn's face whipped right and then left scanning the traffic. Her familiar features panned before me in a slow hypnotic blur. I felt instantly comforted by her small pointy nose, her milky skin and her unmistakable mouth, lips that never fully met in the middle when they were closed. There was always a small diamond-shape space right in the symmetrical center of her mouth as though it had been drawn by a child. I zeroed in on that diamond shape like I had a hundred times before and everything came clear. We were still in Hong Kong, all of us on some silly highway out in the far flung New Territories, near the Chinese border. Warm, buzzy relief oozed through me. Why had it taken me so long to realize this? Hong Kong was the only logical place Lacey Blackburn could be, with those plump diamond lips.

The station wagon swerved left. Look, I thought to myself, we're headed home now, to our house on the coast. Who knows where this dry pop-up place is, and who cares. It's just some crazy part of Asia, some dusty place with fat spiky plants and different looking cows. I was amused by my imagination, excited to tell Holly about all the stupid things. She was still squashed up against me, small and alert, stringy white-yellow hair swirling like candy-floss in front of her face.

The station wagon swooped another big curve left and all of four of us in the back seat leaned sideways. The car dropped off the highway into a drab valley of dirt brown pastures, long-horn cattle penned behind fences, each one looking placid, all of them staring at the road. The ramp down was so steep it made my heart leap alive, like I'd been stone cold dead for a year. I happily gulped the air, thrilled by the wind but even more thrilled to be going home where my dad was surely waiting.

Mrs. Blackburn twisted back and beamed us a quick, broad smile. There was that reassuring diamond space between her lips, but her sunglasses weren't shaped like cat's eyes, they were brown and round and absolutely wrong.

"Welcome to Texas kids!"

The x'd out sound was unmistakable. Hong Kong was gone. This dry pop-up place was for real, our new home, an angry "ex us" sound.

I sunk into myself, slumped beneath pounds of dead expectation. A moment passed. Lungs deflating. Thumb picking. Heads of hair flapping in the wind.

The car slipped into silence for as long as it took for the sun to finally reach the ridge of a faraway hill. It was a new shade of sunset, not mango-colored like it was in Hong Kong, not bleak white either like it was in England. No, this Texan sunset was watery pale. It sucked the color from our cheeks, turned us all grey, like pearly pink light-bulbs were dimming inside each of us.

When the silence became too loud, when our gloom got stuck in a groove that might never end, Mrs. Blackburn boomed us awake:

"Hey, I have gifts for you guys," she shouted from the front of the station wagon. "I was gonna wait until later, but here, have them now."

She reached over to the passenger seat floor and hoisted a large paper bag up and back to us. Many arms reached to receive it.

"What do you say?" my mother said from her darkened corner of the car.

"Thank you," Holly and I chimed on cue, one part happy, three parts tired.

My mother sounded tired too. She studied our presents from her shadowy corner, subtracting from, not adding to our excitement. Jane was awake again, her black eyes blinking, slowly up, slowly down. She was happily sucking on her pacifier, oblivious and content.

"A doll!" Holly said with genuine pleasure pulling her gift from a skin of flowery paper. She lifted the box close to her face and peered through a plastic window cut into the cardboard packaging. I leaned into Holly's shoulder and pulled the box down so I could see too. Strapped inside, flat against the back of the box was a brittle woman with white-yellow hair tied in two long bunches.

"The doll's got a tennis racket and there's a net," I said pointing to a packet of accessories. "It's Tennis Player Barbie."

"Let go," Holly said shoving me with her shoulder.

Meanwhile, my mother tore at the paper wrapping Jane's large round gift. A hook-shaped horn popped free.

"Look Jane, it's a cow just like the ones out the window," Holly shouted.

"Mooooooooo!" I added for effect.

Jane turned her bobbly head toward me and smiled a loose gummy smile. A mouthful of wet spilled over her lip and she smiled even more. My mother pulled the soft toy away just in time to avoid the saliva.

My gift felt solid. I enjoyed the heft of it. It helped me escape from my idiotic hopes of a moment ago. It felt like something real to look forward to, made me feel appreciated and more of a boy. But I didn't know what it was, even with the paper off. It was a rectangle-shaped box made of wood, both sides covered in a slick of shiny brown and white squares.

"It opens!" Mrs. Blackburn yelled.

And so it did. The rectangle was hinged. I pulled it apart and the box transformed itself into a chess board. Underneath the slick checkered top, in the belly of the box sat two tight fitting wedges of sea-green foam, one either side of the box's hinges. In each bed of foam an individual chess piece was pressed precisely into its own unique hole. One set brown, the other an ivory cream, each piece carved out of smooth weathered stone. Not stone upon closer inspection. The pieces were plastic, stained in some way to make them look old.

"It's a chess set!" Mrs. Blackburn shouted. "Do you play?"

"Thank you," I said again, too shy to add anything else.

"You're welcome."

I sat back astonished that someone, Lacey Blackburn, thought I was old enough and clever enough to play chess. I had never played before and I didn't want to admit it. I knew not to say so, but I didn't want to learn. I liked playing snakes and ladders with my grandmother, even boring old tiddly-winks. This gift, this chess set seemed substantial, it felt meaningful. I didn't want it and I felt ashamed.

"Okay kids!" Mrs Blackburn shouted. "Five more minutes. Almost there!"

Darkness had fully filled the car by now but I was still able to study the chess board's foam-filled underneath, noticing a new detail every time we shot through the misty white shine of a street lamp. I was comforted by each piece tucked so perfectly into its soft foamy home, a hole carved just right for a knight, a king and a queen.

I began to pry out a piece shaped like a horse, the only piece that looked friendly. But I changed my mind and pressed it back into the foam. I ran my hand over all of the pieces instead. I let their solid shapes massage the flat of my palm. A rogue fingertip pressed into the sea-green foam and I felt it slowly swell back to normal. I liked that feeling. I liked how something so firm could regain its shape. I pressed my finger into it again, deeper this time. The foam quickly flooded back up to my fingertip the same as before. It felt like magic.

I shut the chess set with a loud magnetic snap and squirmed away from Holly who was happily bending her stiff tan doll. I turned away from Jane, turned away from my mother and Mrs. Blackburn and all the crunchy chatter that was now filling the car. I twisted myself all the way around so that I was sitting cross-legged on the seat facing the car door. Then I leaned into the window and let my forehead fall against the cool firm of the glass, let the full weight of my head rest there. My reflection flickered in front of me for a short shiny moment, freckled skin, small nose, straw-colored hair. Then a puff of cloudy breath on the glass chased me away.

I watched the white mist shrink at its edges bit by bit. I wondered what made condensation happen, then I wondered about the strange shapes shifting behind the fogged up glass.

Once my breathy fog was all the way gone I saw Texas for the very first time. And there it was, still rushing by, mile after mile of American sand.

In Passing

Rose Tawy

the sky now is a soft gray—
the sea fog is still hours from burning off
and the clouds have not yet decided if
    they will rain
a gull picks at the remnants of
    a styrofoam box of leftovers
and I briefly think of mallards caught
    in clear plastic rings
    still swimming but more slowly now,
    turning sometimes to bite at the ties
    then paddling on, encumbered
though gulls seem to me a sturdier bird
and so I leave him to his meal
he is eyeing me anyway, halfway between
    gorging on his winnings and flight

If I Could

Michael Moynihan

If I could untie my blue hands
I could watch the watchless morning with you.
My eyes could become watchful:
a hummingbird's scarlet cursive
over white flowering bush and gone.

If I could untie my throat
I could listen to the sounds
your mother made as you speak.
My ears could grow attentive:
a mockingbird's awe,
its full countless trill.

About the Editors

SHADAB ZEEST HASHMI'S *Baker of Tarifa*, a book based on the history of interfaith tolerance in Al Andalus (Muslim Spain), won the 2011 San Diego Book Award for poetry. Her poems have been nominated for the Pushcart prize multiple times, translated into Spanish and Urdu, and have appeared in *Poetry International, Vallum, Nimrod, The Bitter Oleander, The Cortland Review, The Adirondack Review, Hubbub, RHINO, Journal of Postcolonial Writings, Spillway,* and are forthcoming in *Prairie*
Schooner, Drunken Boat, and other places. She represents Pakistan on *UniVerse: A United Nations of Poetry*, and has taught in the MFA program at San Diego State University as a writer-in-residence. She is a guest columnist for *3 Quarks Daily*. *Kohl and Chalk* is her new book of poems.

JIM RULAND is a veteran of the U.S. Navy, author of the short story collection Big Lonesome, and curator of the Southern California-based reading series Vermin on the Mount, now in its tenth year. *Giving the Finger: Risking It All to Fish the World's Deadliest Sea*, co-authored with the Scott Campbell, Jr. of Discovery Channel's Deadliest Catch, was published in April. His novel, *Forest of Fortune*, will be published by Tyrus Books in August.

Contributors

SCOTT BARBOUR is an editor and writer in San Diego. He is a member of San Diego Writers, Ink, and a regular at Thursday Writers. His stories have appeared in previous volumes of *A Year in Ink* and in the anthology *Writings on the Wall*.

SHANNON BATES is a musician and writer originally from Fair Oaks, California, currently living in San Diego. She plays saxophone and flute in many genres. A few handfuls of her stories and poems appear in small journals and anthologies, but her forte is writing novels that refuse to reach completion.

DR. LYNN BEMILLER has been practicing medicine in San Diego for more than 20 years. Her essay, *Family Heroes* was published in Annals of Internal Medicine in April 2013. She is enrolled in Stanford University's Online Writing Certificate Program and is working on her first novel.

CHRISTIAN BENAVIDES is a senior at San Diego State University, majoring in English. His love for writing stems from countless hours spent with Ray Bradbury and Edgar Allan Poe. He hopes to publish his writing one day and inspire people as he has been inspired by many.

MARISOL BENTER wants nothing more than to retreat to the redwoods with her Smith-Corona typewriter and her Norwegian Forest Cat Woodstock.

CORI BROWN received her M.A. in English (2009) and M.F.A. in Creative Writing (2010) from National University. Most of her poems and story ideas live in her head but are constantly fighting to get committed to paper. She lives in Poway with her two dogs, Penny and Bridgette.

REBECCA CHAMAA will be starting a MFA program in poetry in March of 2014 at UC Riverside. She has been published in *Pearl, A Year in Ink, Volume 6, Voicewalks, Serving House Journal*, and others. She lives in San Diego with her husband of sixteen years.

ANTHONY CONWRIGHT is a content writer for the literary blog, *Verse and Memoir: Pros from a Secular Humanist*, a site dedicated to fiction, poetry, non-fiction, and the critique of religion. He also teaches sixth grade Humanities at High Tech Middle Media Arts.

CATHERINE DARBY'S work has been published in *The Muse Strikes Back: A Poetic Response by Women to Men, The Temple, The Long Island Quarterly*, and *5x7: A New York Anthology*. She was a Bread Loaf Writers' Conference participant, grant recipient of the Italian-American Foundation, and an editor for *Vox Populi* Anthology of the Seattle Poetry Festival. She lives in San Diego with her husband and two sons.

MARY BETH DODSON is an artist and writer of human interest stories. With the proceeds of her book of poetry, she spent ten days painting in Monet's garden in Giverny, France. After visiting Coronado for many years, she decided to move to San Diego. Every day is one of discovery.

Moving to San Diego in 2005 and reigniting a devotion for writing, **TERRI DUGAN** is a member of San Diego Writers, Ink and Terrence Crow, Jr. Writer's Cooperative. Terri is lucky in love and lucky in motherhood. She is a reformed pessimist, with lapses. *Smackdown* is her first published piece.

TYLER DUNNING is a Montana native. Tyler has revered adventure from a young age. This sentiment has led him around the world; his current goal is to visit every U.S. national park. His occupations have ranged from professional wrestling to academia, but at his core he's a writer. Find his work at www.tylerdunning.com.

MEGAN ELLIOTT'S writing has appeared in *A Year In Ink, Vol. 5, City Works, Pacific Review*, and other publications. She lives in San Diego.

JUDY GERACI is a writer and educator living in San Diego. *You See 'Ums* is part of her continuing Tri-City collection of short stories.

RACHEL GREENBERG moved to San Diego in 2012, directly after graduating from the Johns Hopkins University in Baltimore. While supporting herself as a professional content writer, she has stayed active in fiction writing. *Heavy Summer* was influenced by M.R. James and by an interest in journalistic writing.

JILL G. HALL is an artist and writer who owns Inspirations Gallery next to The Ink Spot at NTC. She is a past president of San Diego Writers, Ink. Her poetry has been published in *A Year in Ink, Serving House Journal*, and *Wild Women, Wild Voices.* www.jillghall.com.

JUDITH HANSEN received her MFA from University of Southern California in acting and has performed professionally on stage and screen in New York City and Los Angeles. Her play *The Voice Lesson* was a finalist in Ensemble Studio Theatre's One-Act.

STACEY JOHNSON studied English Literature and Creative Writing at The College Cross in Worcester, MA. She teaches high school English and is currently working on a collection of stories. She is the proud mother of Grace, a four-year-old wonder.

SYLVIA LEVINSON'S poetry life began in 1992 when she worked at the Old Globe Theatre for several years. She is the author of *Spoon* (Finishing Line Press, 2013) and *Gateways* (Caernarvon Press, 2005). Publications include: *Blue Arc West, City Works, A Year in Ink, Magee Park, Christian Science Monitor, The Reader,* and *Serving House Journal.* She believes 'retirement' is an active verb.

FRED LONGWORTH restores vintage audio components for a living, and refuses to follow popular ideological drummers, which antagonizes those marching in jackboots. His poems have appeared in numerous journals, including *Able Muse, California Quarterly, City Works, Comstock Review, Pearl, Rattapallax, Spillway,* and *Stirring.*

Born in Sacramento, CA, **CODY MAURO** studies English at San Diego State University, and in the fall of 2014, will be participating in an MFA program at a still undecided school. He enjoys writing of all forms and genres—fiction, poetry, even literary analysis—and is currently working on a fantasy novella.

VICTORIA MELEKIAN has been published in *Valparaiso Fiction Review, Serving House Journal, Word Riot, Survivor's Review, A Year in Ink, Magee Park Poets, Pearl,* and *ONTHEBUS.* Her story, "What I Don't Tell Him" aired on NPR. She has twice won a San Diego Book Award. For more, visit www.victoriamelekian.com.

MICHAEL MOYNIHAN lives and writes in La Mesa, CA.

UNA NICHOLS HYNUM is grateful for summers at Idyllwild poetry workshops and one week at Squaw Valley Community of Writers, but her main source of inspiration comes locally, from weekly sessions with some of San Diego's best poets: Live Oaks Poets, Blue Stocking Poets, and from classes and readings at Oasis, Magee Park, and San Diego Writers, Ink.

CLAUDIA POQUOC has a BA in Education and additional study in Modern and Contemporary Poetry. She hosts a women's poetry revision group called *Bluestockings* after the earlier poets in England. Claudia teaches poetry through the California Poets in the Schools (CPITS) and Border Voices Poetry Project. Her published song and poetry book, *Becomes Her Vision,* includes a CD. Her poems appear in anthologies throughout San Diego and other publications.

ANDREW PRINTER is an artist and writer living in San Diego. A previous story, *Emoticon,* was included in the anthology *The Frozen Moment: Contemporary Writers on the Choices that Change Our Lives (2012).*

DEBORAH RAMOS, a native of Ocean Beach, has been evolving as an artist and writer since high school. Deborah's award winning poetry has appeared in publications such as *Sage Woman Magazine*, the *San Diego Poetry Anthology 2010, Rattlesnake Press*, and *Gypsy Daughter's Brown Bagazine.* Deborah's poems are sensual and visceral, using language full of vision and attitude.

NED RANDOPH received his MA in graduate creative writing at Eastern Michigan University, where he also taught English. A native of Louisiana, he worked as a speechwriter for the Mayor of New Orleans and spent a decade as a news reporter. He is currently a PhD student at UCSD.

JUDY REEVES is a writer, teacher, and writing practice provocateur who has published four books on the craft including *A Writer's Book of Days*. Her next book, *Wild Women, Wild Voices*, will be published by New World Library in spring 2015. Meantime, the unfinished novel still keeps her up nights.

LAURIE RICHARDS practices law and writing surrounded by chaparral on the mountains framing her valley. Her muse is a coyote that trots through her garden every morning.

JESSE ROBINSON was born in the Alaskan wild and raised by a pack of wolves. At the age of 18 he was admitted to SDSU with an American Grey Wolf Protection Act scholarship. He lives in San Diego with his 3/4 wolf children, humor and satire.

JENNIFER RUBY is a poet and high school English teacher. She was raised in Claremont and was educated at UC Davis and CSU Sacramento. Currently, she is a student in the UCLA Extension Writer's Program and is at work on a YA novel.

AMERICA SALVATORE, a native of Brooklyn, NY, is a poet, accomplished makeup artist, animal lover, and avid motorcycle rider. She moved to California 15 years ago and now resides in San Diego. She is currently pursuing her love of poetry.

NANCY SANDWEISS wrote doggerel as a child in Detroit and learned to write poetry in Mary Harker's OASIS class in San Diego. She also credits Bluestocking Poets for sage advice and encouragement.

NIKI SHAFFER is a former prosecutor with the California Department of Justice. She is a hospice volunteer, and an avid reader and writer. Niki lives in San Diego with her husband, Don. This is her first published piece. It is dedicated to the cherished memory of Niki's much missed mother.

DAVID J. SCHMIDT is a freelance writer, folklore researcher, multi-lingual translator, and home brewer in San Diego, CA. He speaks eight languages, and has published writings in English and Spanish. In addition to co-authoring the *Daily Book of Art* and *The Daily Book of Photography*, he is the author of the erotica-romance parody, *Pirates of the Danube*.

ROSE TAWY grew up walking in the Henry Cowell redwoods, and enjoys pondering roots that yield such strength and stature. When she is not counting rings, she shares her love for reading with San Diego high school and college students.

BRIAN THEDELL lives in East County, answering the muse's call as he can. He lives with Adrian and an adorable Chihuahua named Xero.

About San Diego Writers, Ink

San Diego Writers, Ink, serves as a hub for the literary community, promotes literature, provides artistic development for writers at all levels, and facilitates artistic collaboration. A 501(c)(3) nonprofit organization, SDWI offers classes, groups, workshops, readings, and other literary events at The Ink Spot and other locations throughout San Diego County.

San Diego Writers, Ink
www.SanDiegoWriters.org

The Ink Spot
2730 Historic Decatur Rd #202
San Diego, CA 92106
(619) 696-0363

A Year in Ink, an anthology published each year by San Diego Writers, Ink, represents a sampling of our community's most brilliant work. Each volume includes short stories, novel and memoir excerpts, creative nonfiction, satire, flash fiction, poetry, and more. The authors are a diverse group of young and old, new writers and much-published veterans. Several have had work in previous anthologies, most have been published in other literary journals, and a few allow *A Year in Ink* the honor of showcasing their first publication.

Explore the complete *A Year in Ink* collection. Available at our website.

A Year in Ink, Vol. 1 (2008), edited by Thomas Larson
A Year in Ink, Vol. 2 (2009), edited by Sandra Alcosser and Arthur Salm
A Year in Ink, Vol. 3 (2010), edited by Roger Aplon and Jennifer Silva Redmond
A Year in Ink, Vol. 4 (2011), edited by Jericho Brown and Laurel Corona
A Year in Ink, Vol. 5 (2012), edited by Brandon Cesmat and T. Greenwood
A Year in Ink, Vol. 6 (2013), edited by Michael Klam and Anthony Bonds
A Year in Ink, Vol. 7 (2014), edited by Shadab Zeest Hashmi and Jim Ruland

Calypso Editions

BASED IN SAN DIEGO. PUBLISHING FINE BOOKS.

Calypso Editions is an artist-run, cooperative press based in San Diego and dedicated to publishing quality literary books of poetry and fiction with a global perspective.

We believe that literature is essential to building an international community of readers and writers and that, in a world of digital saturation, books can serve as physical artifacts of beauty and wonder.

For more information, drop us a line at info@CalypoEditions.org.

The Little Trillogy

by Anton Chekhov

Translated by Boris Dralyuk

Fiction, Bilingual edition

How Much Land Does a Man Need

by Leo Tolstoy

Translated by Boris Dralyuk

Fiction, Bilingual edition

INFO@CALYPSOEDITIONS.ORG | WWW.CALYPSOEDITIONS.ORG

PEN Center USA salutes

A YEAR IN INK
Volume 7

Congratulations!

PEN Center USA is a membership organization that aims to stimulate
and maintain interest in the written word, to foster a vital literary
culture in the western United States, and to defend
freedom of expression around the world.

Join the six hundred published authors, literary community supporters,
students, and booksellers who support our causes today.

WWW.PENUSA.ORG

www.ingramcontent.com/pod-product-compliance
Lightning Source LLC
Chambersburg PA
CBHW070937250626
47159CB00009B/3284